Psychology of Murder
The traits we share with killers

Casey Lytle

Table of Contents

Introduction
Some thoughts about murder

If you were murdered today, who would do it? The chances are between 75% and 85% that you would know the name or at least recognize the face of the person. Each year murders by family, friends, or acquaintances are the most common.

We teach children about "stranger danger" but children are most likely to be injured or killed by a family member than by anyone else.

News reports of school shootings make us fear for the safety of our children at school, but more children are killed by their parents, and many more are killed in car accidents, than from school shootings. In fact, schools are still one of the safest places for children to be during the day. Does that mean we shouldn't be concerned about school shootings and the cognitions which motivate them?

Have you ever wondered what is going on in the mind of someone who commits a mass shooting, or someone who kills their own child? What are the cognitions that can lead to such a choice? It is unfortunately simple to describe and quite uncomfortable to realize how close you can come to that same mental space. But if you want to go there, to know the warning signs, I'm about to take you there.

We assume people who kill must be mentally ill, because how could a "normal" person ever do that. But most murders every year are by "normal" people, in many cases people just like you, who do not believe they could ever be pushed to that point. My goals in this book are to inform you, scare you, and put tools in your mental toolbox to help you understand the dark corners you need to watch for so you will know when you are stepping closer to that edge, closer to a bad choice. A choice you think you would never make, but a choice that in the moment feels rational, satisfying, and deserved. We will look inside the heads of killers, then look at how many of those thoughts and motivations we share every day.

Let's use an example from the other side of the spectrum.

There are people who would never kill, for any reason. Not even to preserve their own life or the life of a loved one. These people usually hold strongly to a religious doctrine and believe their hope of an eternal afterlife rides on not violating the "Thou Shall Not Kill" (or Thou Shall Not Murder) commandment. How could they stand aside and watch a loved one die or allow their own death? It is not hard to understand. They believe fully in an eternal afterlife. To them this life is a blip on the eternal radar, a proving ground to demonstrate you are worthy of an eternal reward. Why would you risk sacrificing eternity to briefly prolong this short life? And why would you rob a loved one of being able to move on to that eternal paradise by prolonging this short life for a few years and possibly robbing yourself of that same reward?

Those people exist, but they are not the majority. For everyone else there is a situation in which you would make the choice to kill and feel justified in the moment of doing it. Whether it counts as murder or not depends on whether the broader culture, and formal law, agree with your justification. If they agree, it is not murder. If they do not agree, it is murder. We mostly agree that murder is the worst crime you can commit, taking away not just the life of a person, but their entire future as well. Yet, it is arguably the crime we most frequently try to excuse.

In the first couple chapters we will start with the basics. The different categories of murder and their definitions, murder statistics over the years and generational trends, the neurology of the homicidal impulse, and our cultural and media obsession with murder. From there we will dedicate individual chapters to the most common categories of murder, studying examples of murderers, their motivations and their cognitions.

It is important to note, when I say we will get into their heads to understand why they do it, I am not doing so to create sympathy for them or forgive what they have done, but to understand the impulse and how close many of us come to that line without crossing it, because it is an important step toward improving our own personal safety and understanding the world around us.

This book is based on the Psychology of Murder class I taught for several years at Eastern Washington University. It is very much a print version of that class, therefore, written in a very conversational, rather than academic, tone. It is also limited in content to what I covered in that class; it is not an encyclopedia of behavioral traits and cognitive progressions of all killers. In each of the chapters covering different categories of murder (such as mass shooters and serial killers) I select a sample who are representative of different categories and different progressions but by no means provide an exhaustive list of examples.

If you are a former student of mine who took the Psychology of Murder class, this will simply be a review, but you will notice something missing from the print version: The timed interjections of dark humor meant to briefly take the edge off and make the class tolerable. That is useful, and to a degree necessary, within the context of in-person presentation to a group, but it does not translate well to print.

If you are ready to take the dive, let's go for a ride!

Chapter One
Murder by Numbers

We need to start with the impact that social media and 24/7 mass media have had on the way you perceive the world today compared to previous decades.

Think about what you know about national and world events in the 1950's. The Cold War, the Red Scare, the Korean War, the McCarthy hearings, Rosa Parks, Brown v the Board of Education, the Cuban Revolution, etc. We know more about those events today than people did at the time because media was very limited in what it covered. Most of what people in the 1950s knew about national and world events came from whatever their local and regional newspapers chose to print, or what short news broadcasts on radio and television chose to air. National news broadcasts on television were mostly 15-minute highlights of key events, not expanding to 30-minutes until the 1960s. Not a lot of time to cover everything going on outside your community. The stories chosen by mass media were intended to appeal to the majority demographic; rarely would stories of interest to minority populations be chosen for national broadcast or publication. You really had no idea of the day-to-day experiences of everyday people outside of those you interacted with directly.

Now imagine we take today's cellphones, social media, and 24/7 cable news and place it in the 1950s. How would our view of that decade be different? We would suddenly be flooded with average people expressing their views and showing us their experiences. We would see videos directly from the scene of events as they took place. Events that in some cases news outlets would limit to local coverage if they had covered it at all. We would be flooded with both information and misinformation of what was going on outside our communities.

You would have heard of the suspicious fire at the "Reform School" outside Wrightsville, Arkansas in 1959 that killed 21 African American boys (Encyclopedia of Arkansas). Social media would have talked about the difference between white reform schools, where marketable trades such as welding and carpentry were taught, compared to Black reform schools where people were used essentially as slave labor in agriculture.

You would have heard about Junior High School student Billy Ray Prevatte, who in 1956 shot three teachers, killing one, while roaming the school hunting for the Principal who had earlier reprimanded him for failing to turn in an assignment (Madera Tribune, 1956). Without social media and mass media you would have only heard about it if you lived in Maryland; if you lived anywhere else it was probably not mentioned in any radio or television news, or chosen as a story in local or regional newspapers. You might have thought school shootings did not happen at all unless one happened locally. It was not until the Columbine shootings in 1999 that mass media began reporting school shootings nationally, regardless of how many people were injured or killed.

Social media in the 1950s would have made you more aware of child abductions, domestic violence, child abuse, sexual assault, abortion, racial and gender inequality, and political corruption. Subjects which were relegated to local gossip and mostly ignored by media to keep us thinking our streets were safe, everyone happily followed social norms, and bad things only happened to bad people.

Keep these things in mind as we go through the book if you find yourself falling into the trap of thinking "what is wrong with people today? People didn't do this in my day." Yes, they did. You were simply less likely to hear about it.

The statistics in this chapter come from the Centers for Disease Control (https://www.cdc.gov/nchs/fastats/homicide.htm) and the FBI Uniform Crime Report (https://ucr.fbi.gov/crime-in-the-u.s/). Together they are the most extensive resources available today for crime statistics.

Let's start with a statistic many people find surprising. In the United States, the decades of the 1970s and 1980s which many people look upon nostalgically as better times, were the peak of almost every category of crime in our lifetimes. Between 1972 and 1997 the number of murders per year never dipped below 18,000. Between 1979 and 1995 the number of murders per year was over 20,000 fourteen times.

Compare that to 2015, a year in which the number of murders per year had jumped from the previous year. There were 15,883 murders in 2015, up from 14,164 in 2014, a low not seen since the 1960s, when the U.S. population was much lower.

In the mid-1990s the murder rate, and crime overall, began to gradually decline in the United States, finally dipping below 20,000 in 1996, and below 18,000 by 1998. After an uptick in the early 2000's, peaking with 17,030 in 2006, the downward trend continued, ending with the low of 14,164 in 2014. The fewest murders in a year since 1968. Think about it. The U.S. in 2014, with a population of 317 million had roughly the same number of murders as the U.S. in 1968 when the population was 200 million. More people, less crime.

What happened to bring about this change? An entire generation of readers won't like this, but it was the aging of the baby boomers. As the boomers aged into the primary adult demographic, age 18 to 39, they brought with them a wave of crime and social problems which only declined as they aged out of that range and Gen X and Millennials replaced them. Both those generations have produced lower rates of every category of crime compared to the boomers (Spelman, 2021). Not to deny that Boomers broke down many social norms which needed broken and brought much positive change, but there was an undeniable downside to that big generation as well.

The post-Boomer news is not all good. The post-Boomer generations have lower rates of murder overall, but they have also been the generations to see an increase in mass shootings and school shootings (we will address some of the reasons in the chapter on Mass shooter). After murder hit a low point in 2014 the number of murders per year began to climb again, jumping over 20,000 in 2020 for the first time since 1995. As of this writing in 2022 it is too early to pin down specific causes, but the statistics reveal most of the increase is coming from the largest cities. Rural communities experiencing financial distress have also ticked up over that time. It is also not hard to assume the political divide which exploded in the U.S. in 2016 and again in 2020 (along with the COVID-19 outbreak and shutdowns) contributed to the increase. But like the drop in the mid-90s, it takes several years to get enough data to see a consistent pattern.

Who is most likely to kill you?

We think of murder as a crime committed during the act of another crime. Only criminals commit murder, right? In any given year between 75% and 85% of all murders are "family/friend/acquaintance" murders. Meaning, if you were murdered today, you would most likely know the name, or at least recognize the face, of the person who killed you. You might assume most murders are by people with a criminal mentality or mental illness, therefore if no one you know fits that criteria you must be safe, right? In chapter three we will cover the cognitive and emotional influences which can lead spontaneously to murder in the absence of a criminal history or mental illness. For now, suffice it to say almost anyone can be driven to an emotional extreme in which, for a brief period, they are capable of either intentionally or unintentionally killing another person. It is unfortunately very common.

It runs counter to who we are socialized to trust, but as we will see in Chapter Five, between birth and adulthood, regardless of your gender the people most likely to kill you are caregivers. In adulthood, if you are a woman, you are more likely to be killed by a current or former intimate partner than a stranger, and if you are pregnant the risk is even greater (Wallace, et al., 2021).

Our fascination with murder

As I said in the introduction, we mostly agree that murder is the worst crime you can commit but is also the one we most frequently bend the rules to excuse. In Chapter Five we will see how the French Penal Code of 1810 set the stage for the "Crime of Passion" defense when a husband kills a partner who was either cheating or suspected of cheating, and several passages in the Bible laid the foundation for endorsing "Honor Killing" of family members if they were perceived as violating moral rules or in any way dishonoring the family (specifically the father).

Across the United States various laws based on the Castle Doctrine or "Stand your ground" laws allow private citizens to kill people for offenses which the legal system do not consider death-penalty offenses. Stealing a lawn mower from someone's garage is a relatively minor offense if caught by the police, but in many jurisdictions a homeowner might be protected under the law for killing the person. Many "stand your ground" definitions do not require the threat of death when using lethal force on someone perceived to be a threat. Some jurisdictions do specify a "duty-to-retreat" requirement, meaning if you have a chance to escape without harm you are obligated to take it rather than use lethal force, but very few states have that clause, and all of them exclude the requirement to escape if you are in your own home.

This is why "no knock" warrants are so controversial, especially when police are at the wrong address. By law, if someone busts down your door in the night you have the legal right to shoot them to death without having to identify them first. In fact, by the definition of most Stand Your Ground laws, if someone points a gun at you (or anything you perceive as a gun) you have the right to shoot them to death.

In February 2012 "Neighborhood Watch" volunteer George Zimmerman in Sanford, Florida, spotted 17-year-old Trayvon Martin going through the neighborhood. Zimmerman reported him to police as a suspicious person, then chose to confront him. An altercation ensued and Zimmerman shot Martin, killing him. Zimmerman claimed self-defense and the Stand Your Ground law as his excuse even though he initiated the encounter.

November 2007 in Pasadena Texas, 61-year-old Joe Horn spotted two men breaking into his neighbor's house. He called 9-1-1 to report it, and announced he was going to stop them himself. Despite multiple pleas by the 9-1-1 operator to wait for police, Horn went out and confronted them. When they entered his yard, he shot them multiple times, killing both.

In principle, Stand Your Ground is a valid consideration for citizens to protect themselves from harm, but in practice it relies too much on the *perception* of threat rather than any actual threat that a reasonable person would be expected to recognize. It has exonerated people acting in genuine self-defense when previous laws would have put them at risk of jail time for defending their lives but has also been misused due to unintended technicalities. In Florida, drug dealers and gang members have sometimes successfully used it as defense, and it does not always favor the innocent. For example, if someone comes up to you in Florida and initiates a fight, and you feel threatened enough to draw your weapon, you can use the Stand Your Ground defense if you kill them, but because you are also a threat to them, they can use it as a defense if they kill you.

How we perceive killers

How we label or perceive a killer starts with whether we perceive the killing as justified. This is not always clear-cut and universal; it can vary by situation and group identity. The most obvious example in media today are police shootings. There is less controversy when police have killed someone who was an obvious threat to public safety, but more controversy when they kill someone less for public threat and more out of self-defense. The public perception is that police, as part of the job they accept, are supposed to accept a greater risk to their personal safety than what would be expected from a private citizen. Such a view is understandable given that we expect police (and first responders in general) to run toward the very people and situations that the rest of us would be justified in fleeing. Police are also the armed authority with the job of directly interacting with citizens. The National Guard interacts with citizens during times of social or national crisis, and the formal branches of the military are expected to rarely, if ever, play an enforcement role with private citizens, so both the National Guard and other branches of the military operate under different expectations. For example, no one would expect a solider to refuse to enter combat because they feel it is a risk to their safety, or to refuse an order because they know they have little chance of surviving.

The reality is police are not robots. They do receive training meant to give them greater skills than the general population in handling conflict, and they are expected to take greater risks to self than what would be expected from the general public, but they are also human and have the same survival instincts as anyone else. Police are sent into dangerous situations, but unlike the military, the police are rarely sent into situations in which they are expected to risk certain death to achieve a goal. They can consider personal risk when making decisions on the job. It is this decision-making where objective judgment after-the-fact can clash with subjective judgment in the moment and create controversial outcomes.

Individual citizens who kill are subject to similar judgment. As I mentioned earlier, if society and law agree with your reasons for killing someone, it is not murder. If they do not agree, then it is. If they are uncertain, or there might be extenuating circumstances, then it goes to court. Therefore, there are "degrees of murder" based on intent.

Some cases might seem obvious to groups who identity in some way with the person who committed the killing, but other groups might take an entirely different view. During the unrest in Kenosha, Wisconsin in August 2020, 17-year-old Kyle Rittenhouse killed two people and wounded another. Some perceived his act as murder, others perceived it as self-defense. In that case public opinion was not influenced so much by the objective facts of the event (many comments online took a side before the facts were known), it was how people felt about the protests in general and the protesters specifically.

Once someone is labeled a "murderer" the public perception of them completely changes. They are now evil, a monster, or just "born bad" and nothing about them could ever have been positive. This is the Fundamental Attribution Error, where we assume observed behavior is due to base personality traits rather than the influence of environmental factors. We selectively reinterpret a killer's history to fit the idea that such a person, even when acting "normal" must have always been harboring evil intent. The reality is more frightening. Many more "good" people have the potential to be murderers than we want to believe, and even serial killers spend most of their time *not* killing. Living among people acting and appearing quite normal. Writing someone off as "born bad" is a convenient, and cognitively lazy, bucket to toss someone in as an easy and safe explanation for their behavior. Later we will cover by "born bad" probably does not exist.

But first, let's talk about the role media plays in our perception, understanding, and stereotypes around murder.

Chapter Two

Murder and Media

Every branch and genre of media have their subgroups dedicated to our obsession with murder.

Do a quick search of movies about serial killers and you will get over 500 results (Internet Movie Database).

Murder mysteries are among the most common media in literature, film and television. Even "Action Comedies" will often include murder. In the 1984 action-comedy Beverly Hills Cop, the best friend of Eddie Murphy's character Axel Foley is executed on-screen as the motivation for Foley's desire to pursue the murderers. It was at the time considered a disturbing scene for a film that most viewers went in to expecting a comedy.

True Crime television programs and podcasts are some of the most obsessively viewed programs. A google search for the phrase "true crime" brings up more than 85 million results, and it is considered a cultural norm that women are especially attracted to programs about serial killers (more on that in a moment).

Despite decades of attempts by parent groups to limit the amount of violence on television, the TV-ratings system implemented in 1997 meant to allow viewers to avoid violent or sexualized programming had the opposite effect, opening the door for an increase in both. It also drew attention to the lingering Puritanical roots of the United States in that greater effort has been made to limit sexual content on television than violent content. Why such a difference? Sex is something most people will experience in their lives and is a natural part of the human life cycle, necessary for perpetuating the species. We have an entire set of hormones and neurotransmitters dedicated to driving the reproductive impulse, but violence against self is something we hope to never experience. Shouldn't sex be more accepted than murder? Viewers believe sex is more common on television than violence primarily because they have habituated to violence and do not notice it as readily. Culturally and historically violence carries harsher punishment, but sex has generated a greater volume of moral rules in an attempt to regulate and control the behavior.

We can answer that question by looking at one subset we just mentioned: Women being attracted to stories of serial killers. First, it is true; women are more attracted to True Crime in general, and serial killers specifically than men (Vicary, 2010), but the reason has multiple components:

- It creates a sense of relief seeing the guilty person caught.
- It creates a sense of preparedness. Seeing the tactics of the killer makes the viewer/reader/listener feel more prepared to avoid something similar.
- There is a sense of justice seeing the person caught, especially if they were ultimately executed.

Shouldn't these things be true of men too? Yes. So why does it impact women more? Because women live day-to-day under a greater threat of violence than men. A man going out walking the dog is generally not worried about someone grabbing him or attacking him, but women must be more consciously aware of their surroundings almost all the time, especially when they are alone or there are few others around. It is argued that this perception of threat triggers the evolutionary survival instinct and drives the fascination with crime programs.

This impacts women more than men in general, but anything which elevates your awareness of threat, regardless of your demographic, will influence attraction to stories of violence. If you live in a high-crime area, or have personally been victim of violence, or had someone close to you become a victim of violence your perception of threat will be elevated and, in theory, your self-preservation instincts will drive the need for preparedness. This can involve a fascination with True Crime stories, a need for greater self-protection (such as acquiring weapons or learning physical self-defense), or in some cases, having nightmares about being the victim of violence or crime. All of these are thought to be ways the brain prepares itself in advance for the possibility of experiencing a threat to survival.

One of the natural cognitive progressions of this obsession is an increasing confidence (sometimes over-confidence) in your ability to identify a threat and defend yourself. Watch enough True Crime stories about murderers and serial killers who were caught, and how they were caught, and you will start to feel more confident that you could spot them and avoid them. The cognitive database of crime stories you have stored will cue up any time you hear about unsolved or otherwise mysterious cases, and with it will come your own ideas of who did it and how it was done. In the age of social media, stories of unsolved cases generate a tremendous amount of interest and huge web traffic. The 2021 case of Brian Laundrie and Gabby Petito, in which Laundrie returned home to Florida in the couple's van without Petito and refused to talk to anyone about where she was or what had happened. By no surprise this caused the case to quickly become a trending topic online, creating a wide range of speculation. Theories ranged from Laundrie being traumatized because he accidentally killed Petito and returned home in a kind of catatonic auto-pilot state, to the extreme that he was a serial killer who had also killed two other women who had been found murdered around the same time in an area where Laundrie and Petito were known to have camped. Such speculation led to suspicion of cover-ups when Laundries' body was found in a nature reserve not far from his parent's home and the case was considered solved and closed.

In this case the online True Crime sleuths and the publicity around the case helped authorities locate Petito's body. As the story spread through social media, people who had seen the Laundries or their van posted videos, and one, showing the van near a specific camping area, eventually led searchers to Petito's body.

In 2013, 26-year-old Brandon Lawson of San Angelo Texas went missing after leaving home near midnight following an argument with his girlfriend. His truck ran out of gas roughly 20 miles out of town, he made multiple calls to his brother asking for gas and claiming he was being chased. His girlfriend and brother claim he was under the influence of meth at the time. After making multiple short and erratic calls to his brother and to 9-1-1 the calls abruptly stopped. His truck was found but he was never seen again. Police assumed he had left the area, others assumed he had been in a manic and paranoid state due to the drug effects and probably got seriously hurt and died from exposure in the 100-degree temperatures the following days. The latter theory was supported by the discovery in February 2022 of clothing and human remains discovered a mile from where the truck had been abandoned.

Although on the surface a straightforward case, the poor quality and frantic content of the 9-1-1 call led to speculation there were others with him, some claiming they could hear another voice on the call and even gunshots. Others speculated he had been killed by either his girlfriend or brother and they staged the story of the truck running out of gas. Still others claimed he staged his own death to escape legal trouble.

Possibly the most popular and well-known "true crime murder mystery" is the still-unsolved case of JonBenet Ramsey, found murdered in her parent's basement in December 1996. Immediately suspicion centered on the parents and brother, but over time nearly everyone who had contact with the family have been suspected. This case drew attention right away because early reports did not seem to fit together. The parents reported finding a ransom note when they realized she was missing. While police were at the house the father went down into the basement and found her body in a windowless room. He brought it upstairs, therefore potentially disturbing the crime scene (she had been sexually assaulted but was fully clothed when the father brought her upstairs, and why would a kidnapper leave a ransom note when the body was in the house?). The ransom note turned out to be written on stationary and with a pen from the mother's room. There were too many pieces that did not fit, and as the investigation went on the parents become less cooperative. It was a magnet for true-crime enthusiasts.

In all these cases, speculations come from comparing elements of the case to other True Crime events in order to fill in the blanks or offer alternative explanations when pieces of the story do not appear to make sense.

Is it wrong to use previous crimes to speculate on current unsolved crimes? Not at all. Police do it all the time, which is why the people closest to the victim are the first who need to be cleared. Statistically they are the most frequent culprits, so it makes sense they are the first you investigate. Most people understand this and are cooperative, therefore an uncooperative relative will always generate suspicion.

But let's bring this back around to an earlier point: Feeling confident you could spot the signs of danger and avoid it. This creates the risk of producing overconfidence, and overconfidence can lead to being less cautious and making mistakes. For example, movies and television have glamorized guns as an ultimate form of intimidation and protection far beyond their real defensive value. This is sometimes labeled as "Action Movie Syndrome" in which people think, like in fictional media, the good person always has superior speed and aim, and the bad person will always conveniently pause at the right moment or be slow and inaccurate so the hero can be victorious. This could cause someone in the real world to take an unnecessary chance, such as confronting an armed person rather than seeking cover, fleeing, or avoiding the situation altogether. Any time a homeowner successfully defends themselves from intruders it gets a lot of media attention. But what about the homeowners who failed in defending themselves? Those are not immediately reported as failures because there is no initial indication of the attempt. They are usually reported as "Body found; robbery suspected." There is no one around to tell the tale of what happened, and quite often there is no sign the homeowner tried to defend themselves with a weapon because the robber took the weapon with them after killing the homeowner (guns are very valuable burglary targets). It can be months before investigators determine what happened, and by then it is old news of little or no interest to media.

In True Crime programs, especially documentaries about serial killers, this problem is compounded by the choice of images being shown. Media usually chooses pictures which make the killers look unhinged or dangerous, rather than showing images of how they might look if you encountered them on the street. In fact, the public is often upset when media shows very typical smiling pictures of murderers. They want the image to fit the crime. This makes people overconfident in their ability to spot a dangerous person. They believe "you can see it in their eyes." We will cover this problem in greater detail in the chapter on serial killers.

There is another demographic we need to recognize who are also attracted to crime, murder, and horror in general: People seeking the emotional ride. It varies on where you live, but in the technologically advanced nations of the world this is the safest time to live in all human history. We live mostly very sanitized and protected day-to-day lives where the greatest immediate threats are car accidents and financial woes. Most of us never personally experience the threat of murder other than through media, and our perception that the world is worse today does not come from direct experience, it comes from mass media and social media giving us access to the world in a way we did not have in previous generations.

Think of it this way, if you narrowly escaped death at the hands of a serial killer, you might not like documentaries about serial killers getting away with it. It hits too close to home emotionally and could trigger powerfully negative emotions. The attraction is greater if it is something you have never experienced. You can experience the terror vicariously through the images on the screen, words on the paper, the voice on the podcast, but you can safely turn it off and go on with your life afterward, like experiencing the terror of a rollercoaster but being able to step off afterward and walk away, whereas someone who survived a plane crash might have a very bad reaction to the same sensation.

The theory is that evolution has prepared us to experience life threats and frightening emotions as part of our survival instinct, but lacking these in our day-to-day lives, we seek them out through media.

During its first season in 1995, the television program "ER" on NBC aired an Emmy Award winning episode called "Love's Labor Lost" in which (Spoiler ahead) a pregnant woman dies during childbirth. It is a heart-wrenching episode which is painful to watch (in fact, if you have had the real-life experience of losing a loved one in similar circumstances it is impossible to watch; possibly even emotionally dangerous). The majority of the audience was able to experience this heartbreak and trauma over the course of an hour, then turn off the television and return to a life where the emotion lingers but the event is not impacting your life, you are not living with the reality of it. This is what we mean when we say the brain is preparing for handling a trauma like that without experiencing it, and that is what draws us to disaster, horror, and murder in media. There is an instinctual draw toward it which is stronger in those who experience little threat or trauma in their day to day lives.

Media also helps create and fuel exaggeration, stereotypes, and cultural myths. Contrary to how they are frequently represented in fiction, serial killers are not exceptionally smart, nor routinely evil. They spend 99% of their time living very normal lives. And even when the story is dark enough on its own, we like to make it darker. When someone has engaged in terrible and shocking behavior, any suggestion of other deviant behavior is immediately accepted even in the absence of supporting evidence. During Ted Bundy's reign of terror in the 1970s any gruesome unsolved murder was rumored to be connected to him. The number of people who claim to have encountered him and escaped him has grown larger than the number of people who claim to have attended Woodstock in the 60s. As I mentioned earlier, Brian Laundries' public image quickly escalated from someone who might have accidentally killed his partner, to a serial killer traveling the country hunting victims.

This is nothing new. The Countess Elizabeth Bathory of Hungary spent 25 years using her position to lure, torture and kill young girls from 1585 until her arrest in 1610. As bad as the stories were, they eventually exaggerated to stories of satanic rituals and bathing in the blood of virgins to preserve her youth.

Gilles de Rais was a 15th century commander in the French army, who for a time fought alongside Joan of Arc. He was later accused of murdering children, and some of the claims of what he did would make Jeffrey Dahmer look tame by comparison. Of course there were accusations of occult connections (any time someone does evil things Satan has to somehow be involved), but by the 20th century, historians were beginning to doubt whether he was guilty of any of these crimes or was targeted and falsely accused by enemies wanting to get rid of him.

The **Cultivation Effect** (Gerbner, 1986, 1994) explains how media (both real and fiction) influences our perception of direct experiences with the real world. In a nutshell, our brains are not designed to completely separate media from real-world experiences. Gerbner's initial studies compared subjects who viewed a lot of crime-related television programming to those who did not. The studies found that immersion in crime-related programs led to higher estimates of the subject's local crime rate compared to those who watched less crime-related television. This is not about being able to tell the difference between fiction and reality, it is about the way your brain stores memories of your experiences, both real-world experiences and fictional experiences through media. As you are watching a program you are aware it is fiction, just actors on a screen. But later, when thinking about the personal risks posed by crime in your community your brain very quickly starts accessing all crime-related memory without considering the original source. This results in an "intuitive feeling" of your personal real-life risk that has been partially influenced by fiction. It is the same with emotional responses. The deeper emotional processing areas of our brain do not know or care that the information they are receiving is on a screen, or coming from the pages of a book, they assume everything coming to them is being witnessed by you in the real world, therefore, they deliver emotional responses. That is why, even though you know something is fiction being presented by actors, or simply words on a page, it will still make you sad, or happy, or scared.

If I spent Sunday afternoon watching a horror movie involving little blonde kids possessed by demons, I understand it is fiction. But if I'm leaving for work the next morning and I see little blonde kids standing outside my house, my brain automatically cues up the stored fictional experience to give me an instant chill and sense of threat from those kids. Fiction has influenced my interpretation of a real-world event.

This is why UFO reports did not flourish until the first reports spread through media, and even though the first account was misreported as a "flying saucer" the majority of later sightings reported a saucer shape, and science fiction films created the visual of "flying saucers" which further escalated the reported sightings. When the secret SR-71 "blackbird" spy-plane began flying in the early 60s it created many UFO reports describing it as a "cigar-shaped" object due to its unique shape, dark color, and incredible speed compared to other aircraft of the time. This caused an explosion in reports of cigar-shaped UFOs. Multiple Personality Disorder was extremely rare until the book and film versions of Sybil were released.

News media has this same influence because it does not report common or typical events, it reports rare and uncommon events. Most people have never personally experienced a mass shooting, but through both news media and fictional programming you have stored memories of mass shootings, which can make you believe they are much more likely in your immediate environment. People who live in very safe, low-crime environments can be made frightened of their environment from exposure to crime-related media. When media reports any incidence of an otherwise low-threat risk, it can make the risk seem more common.

In this same way, media can give us false and stereotyped impressions of specific demographics. As I mentioned earlier, news stories will frequently show the most shocking or "evil looking" photos they can find of killers, creating the impression that "you can tell by looking at them" that they are a threat. They will use headlines like "insane killer" and mass shooters are bucketed as "pure evil." Any history of mental health treatment in the killer's history (no matter how brief or inconsequential) will become the focus of causal speculations. In other words, media knows its audience and gives the audience what it wants to hear and see.

If I were to ask a random selection of people to do their best impression of a person with schizophrenia, they will give me a very stereotyped impression because the most common image of schizophrenia comes from movies and television. These are frequently extreme versions of the disorder with statistically rare combinations of symptoms. What do you think of when you think of schizophrenia? Probably visual and auditory hallucinations. Although auditory hallucinations (the brain misinterpreting auditory input from the environment or creating its own signals in the auditory cortex) are fairly common, visual hallucinations only occur in about a quarter of subjects, mostly on the severe end of the spectrum. The most common symptom, and the one most difficult for people to imitate, is disordered thinking.

In movies and television, killers are frequently driven by hallucinations and delusions, assuming schizophrenia even if it is not specified, and schizophrenics overall are often perceived as dangerous (DeMare, 2016) or living in a world dominated by hallucinations. In the film "A Beautiful Mind" (Howard, 2001) Mathematician John Nash was shown experiencing, and being guided by, very vivid visual and auditory hallucinations. It was understandably necessary for the plot and to help the audience visually understand disordered thinking and delusional beliefs, but the real John Nash never experienced visual hallucinations, and only started experiencing auditory hallucinations later in the progression of the disease. His primary symptoms were delusional beliefs. (Spoiler Alert!) In the film Nash thought he was detecting secret Soviet messages in U.S. mass media. The real Nash believed he was receiving mental messages from Aliens telling him to help establish a New World Order (Nasar, 2002).

The disorder which has overtaken schizophrenia in both fictional media and news media as an assumed root of violent behavior is Bipolar Disorder (O'Hern, 2017), especially in television dramas, BPD is frequently used as a plot device to create suspense or make a villain seem particularly unhinged and chaotic. The reality of all mental illnesses, as we will see in chapter four, is that mental disorders more often result in harm to self than harm to others.

Why is it so popular to misrepresent these populations? Because the audience wants it. When bad things happen, the answers are usually complex, but we want quick and easy answers, the "soundbite" answers or, as they are more commonly called in the 2020s, "Tweetable" explanations.

Keep these things in mind as we go forward explaining cognitive influences on behavior, and the environmental and emotional factors that can gradually nudge "normal" people toward murder. Even in the final chapter we will see that serial killers are more likely "made" than "born," but always keep in mind the stereotypes you might have encoded from exposure to media, and how those stereotypes might clash with the real world.

That said, let's take a quick trip into the structure of the brain and how different hard-wired functions will play an important role going forward.

Chapter Three

The Neuroscience and Psychology behind the impulse to kill

With a few exceptions, most murderers started out with the potential to live very typical non-homicidal lives. They might have even felt they did not have the potential of ever killing another person except in self-defense. So, what changed to eventually lead them to murder?

Obviously, there are many variations, but we can separate key components into different categories. Preexisting mental illness will be covered by itself in the next chapter. Let's start with the leading reason that family/friend/acquaintance murders lead all categories: Rage.

It is important to note, and I will come back to this frequently, that no matter how many risk factors are present, no matter how much of a perfect storm is present in personality traits, emotion, and environment, it does not guarantee a person will commit murder. It can come down to something as simple as degree of impulse control at the instant the elements all come together, or delivering a physical blow harder than expected, or a fall that happens to hit a hard blunt object causing a fatal injury. There can be intent to kill which ends up not killing a victim, and intent to harm but not kill which accidentally results in death. As we will see in later chapters, all the factors can be present and still not produce homicide, it is not a perfect science.

When looking at murders committed during rage (or "crimes of passion" which we will discuss in more detail in a later chapter) we start with a "situationist" perspective which sees murder as a product of the situation more than the killer's disposition. Meaning, they might have gone their entire lives without killing someone if not for the perfect storm of situational factors coming together at the right moment.

If someone is more anger prone in general, are they at greater risk of killing someone? Yes. For the simple reason that they tend to experience anger in greater magnitude and in greater frequency, and obviously the more frequently you are angry, the more likely your anger might correspond to the right situational factors.

Let's cover some basics of the brain. I am going to oversimplify a few descriptions and focus on functions that are important to what we are talking about. The brain is divided into four lobes, and each lobe has a right and left half. The frontal lobes (if you guessed they are in front, you are correct) play a major role in impulse control, decision making, and perception of consequence. In the next chapter we will see that many mental illnesses impair these functions, but even in neurotypical people without any cognitive dysfunction we have wide variations in how well our frontal lobes function throughout the day. Many things can disrupt these functions: fatigue, chemical substances, and strong emotions. When someone goes into a rage the frontal lobes do not function as well. You are at greater risk of making poor choices, having difficulty controlling impulses related to those poor choices, and not thinking at all about the consequences of your choices.

The temporal lobes are on the sides, by each ear. In addition to auditory processing they have some fun functions I wish we could get into here, but for our purposes we are interested mostly in the amygdala, a little almond-sized structure within each temporal lobe that plays a role in emotional intensity. If I could fire up your amygdala right now you would experience a noticeable increase in whatever emotion you are feeling right now. If you are feeling a little anxious, the anxiety would erupt into full-blown fear. The amygdala and frontal lobes working together help us regulate and control emotional response. If either is not working properly, we will have trouble controlling our emotions. You can probably guess, since the frontal lobes can experience reduced functioning simply from fatigue or experiencing a strong emotion, then poor frontal lobe function will mean poor emotional control.

You might be wondering, given that the amygdala can fire up a very strong emotion, and the frontal lobes experience a decrease in impulse control and decision-making from strong emotion, what good is that? It's very good from a survival standpoint. It means you will not try to second-guess or impede your fight-flight response if your brain has determined a threat to survival in your immediate environment, you are more likely to react by survival instinct.

The problem is, we can get mad from things that are not a threat to survival, but the parts of your brain that respond to anger do not know that. We can think ourselves into a rage without environmental input, these brain functions assume rage means threat, and threat must be addressed.

Being anger-prone is a risk, but what do you do with that anger? How do you vent it? Do you deal with it internally or do you lash out externally? Do you vent on inanimate objects (punching a wall, kicking a piece of furniture) or do you physically vent on the person who caused your anger? Even if you do not always vent externally, can you feel the frustration building up and *wanting* to vent physically? How do you keep it from physically venting? Let's use an example which might surprise you.

Shaken Baby Syndrome/Abuse Head Trauma (SBS/AHT) refers to the symptoms present when a baby has been violently shaken or received a blow to the head. According to the National Center on Shaken Baby Syndrome (https://www.dontshake.org/) there are around 1,300 cases reported each year, of which 25% die. Of survivors, over 80% experience lifelong symptoms. When you think about Shaken Baby Syndrome you might think of someone holding a baby and violently shaking them repeatedly, which in many cases is true, but all it takes is one strong jerk of the baby while holding it to whip the head and neck enough to produce injury, and this single jerk of the baby is most often the result of a moment of intense frustration venting itself physically. This is why we advise frustrated parents to put the baby down and step away. Pull yourself together before interacting physically with the baby.

This is the same quick frustration impulse that can make someone punch a wall, kick furniture, or strike a person. If you are prone to this, it is important to understand the situational risk and seek out different ways to deal with escalating frustration.

You can see we are not talking about intentional premeditated murder, rather, cases in which a death occurs out of anger without the intent to kill, even if the intent might be to harm.

Intent to harm is an important component. For example, you are in a heated argument with a friend, family member, or partner, frustration and anger are building. One of the driving impulses when people are angering us or hurting us is the drive to hurt them back. In fact, in a moment of anger, throwing a verbal zinger at someone to hurt them emotionally brings with it a little hit of the feel-good neurotransmitter dopamine. In that instant it feels good, even if we might quickly regret it when we see the reaction. If you are prone to physically venting, this outlet is more likely to be physical than verbal, and in the case of chronic abusers, the regret they might feel immediately afterward is often translated into blame on the victim for "making me do it."

This is also why experts advise against spanking as a form of punishment. As much as parents do not want to admit it, most often spanking is less about correcting the child's behavior and more about venting personal frustration over what the child has done. Our brain delivers a chemical reward for hitting them, and we minimize the seriousness of it by diminishing the word "hit" with the word "spank."

In 1992 the news program 20/20 on ABC aired a segment by John Stossel on spanking. It followed several families who used spanking as discipline. Several were very typical of spanking as punishment, but one family created controversy even for the time because it was obvious their spanking was motivated by their mood, not by the children's behavior. More so, the spanking was not making the children's behavior better, it was leading to the children being aggressive with each other.

Of course, the problem with anger is being aware of it as it is building. Here is an example that is way too common. You are trying to bring the temperature down with an anger-prone person, such as saying, "You don't need to get angry," and their reply is "Oh, this isn't angry, you'll KNOW when I'm angry." This is a person who has lost objective perception of their anger. To them "anger" is the extreme; the point where they have lost control. They are not recognizing the early building stages where the anger is observable to others and beginning to influence the situation. If this person's anger is not already causing problems in their interactions with people, it eventually will. In Anger Management this is the stage where we try to focus subjective awareness on the escalating thoughts and feelings, because this is where self-awareness can help prevent escalation.

I mentioned that anger reduces the impulse-control and decision-making functions of the frontal lobes, but an additional risk factor would be if the anger-prone person has poor impulse-control and decision-making even when they are not angry.

Poor impulse control by itself can be a risk factor in the absence of anger issues. But let's look at cognitive factors in general.

Cognitive progression toward murder.

Here we are talking mostly about visualization and fantasy, and how repeated visualization can create familiarity, and familiarity can create acceptance and sometimes lead to the motivation to play out the fantasy.

Have you ever been so angry at someone that you thought about terrible things happening to them? Dying in horrific ways, or maybe you personally killing them? Imagining is not the same as doing, and fantasy is a safe place to play out taboo behaviors. In fact, such fantasies and visualizations are often seen as a route to emotional healing, so long as they decrease over time. This is going to be a key factor later when we talk about progression in mass shooters and serial killers.

There are some behaviors which are so taboo to you that they will make you uncomfortable no matter how frequently you visualize them, but there are others which might become easier to think about over time, and even easy to imagine doing.

The cognitive effects of sexual arousal can serve as an example, because it will specifically be a factor later when we cover the danger of pairing sexual arousal and aggression.

In 2006, researchers Dan Ariely and George Loewenstein published "The Heat of the Moment: The Effect of Sexual Arousal on Sexual Decision Making" in which they took a sample of college-age Cisgender heterosexual males and measured how their acceptance of various sexual behaviors changed when in an aroused state. The subjects were given a visual "sliding scale" to indicate how likely they would be to endorse the behavior, from zero (not at all) to 100 (definitely). The middle score of 50 indicated "probably." The subjects were first tested in a non-aroused state, then again in an aroused state, then a final time in a non-aroused state again. This was to make sure scores returned to the previous non-aroused score, indicating that the change in the arousal condition was due to arousal, not simply due to repeated exposure to the test.

Some of the questions were rather mundane, such as "Do you prefer to have sex with the light on?" The mean (average) score for that question was 50 in a non-aroused state and 52 in an aroused state. Not a statistically significant difference. But then the questions started going into more taboo areas (taboo anyway for college age Cisgender Heterosexual males): Can you imagine having sex with a 50-year-old woman? Average score of 28 when non-aroused (the "no" side of the scoring spectrum), up to an average of 55 in an aroused state (the "probably" part of the scoring spectrum). "Can you imagine being attracted to a 12-year-old girl?" Score of 23 (no) when non-aroused, doubling to 46 (the low side of "probably") in an aroused state. "Would you keep trying to have sex after your date says 'no?'" Average score of 20 non-aroused, jumping to 45 in an aroused state.

Similar studies found the same results, and studies which included other genders found little if any gender difference in the impact of arousal on decision-making. Skakoon-Sparling, Cramer, and Shuper (2016) also found that sexual arousal not only causes changes in sexually risky choices, but impairs decision making in non-sexual choices as well, meaning it is having a global effect on the frontal lobes in all areas of impulse-control, decision-making, and perception of consequence.

I need to emphasize that these answers reflect how desirable or undesirable the actions felt when the subjects were reading them and thinking about them, it does not mean they would do any of them. Visualization and fantasy do not always translate into behavior, but they need to be present for the behavior to have the potential to occur.

These effects explain why people might think, in a non-aroused state, "I would never let anyone film me having sex," but then in the heat of the moment think it sounds erotic or exciting, then possibly regret it later.

What can be frightening is that people are not generally aware of how their perceptions are changing as the hormones and neurotransmitters do their work. The good news is, if you know in advance that these effects can take place, you can anticipate them, and be aware that those desires of the moment might not be what you really want. An easy cognitive self-check is to think "Yeah, this is really tempting right now, but how will I feel about it tomorrow?" Let your "tomorrow self" make the choice.

Also, these effects were in the absence of any other factors known to impair judgement, such as alcohol or strong emotion. Imagine what those factors in combination with arousal could do?

The same is true of aggression. Just as sexual arousal tries to move you in the direction of sexual behavior, an aggressive mood will try to move you toward aggression. Fear wants to flee; rage wants to fight. We are designed by nature to handle physical threats from the environment and respond to them, but we have taken that same instinctual system and attached it to conceptual threats, such as threats to status, or authority, or relationships. Our big oversized brains can interpret words as physical threats and create threat perception where none really exists.

We know how dangerous it is to physically back an animal into a corner and give it no option but to fight. That is very straightforward for the animal. But humans are a species with language, and language carries information and emotion not always reflected in the immediate physical environment. We can feel backed into a corner by words, and the survival instinct will respond in the same way it would to physical threat.

See the potential soup we can create? We have problems of impulse-control, decision-making, and perception of consequence. We have rage fueling possessiveness, or revenge, or a subjective perception of self-defense. These things merely need an opportunity in the environment to erupt, or a single instance of out-of-control rage with the desire to harm, and the result can be murder.

In the mind of someone lashing out in violence, the violence feels justified and the victim deserves it for whatever reason; something they have done, or a perceived threat they represent whether that threat is real or imagined. A strong sense of threat can trigger a fight/flight response, and that response is centered on the moment right now, it does not care about the future.

Think about how you might respond in the following situation: You have caught someone burglarizing your home. You are holding them at gunpoint, waiting for the police to arrive. The person is making no attempt to get away or pose any immediate threat, but they say to you "You know I'll be out in a couple days. And when I get out, I'm coming back and killing every single person in this house. And it won't be pleasant for them." They might be saying it just to scare you into letting them go, or it might be a genuine threat. Do you take the chance that the person is lying, or that you could easily defend your home again if they return? Or is the threat enough that you would pull the trigger and kill them? What if the law in that state does not allow for lethal force simply from a verbal threat?

In a case like this your brain would not be processing the threat as a hypothetical future event, it would process it as an immediate in-the-moment threat, and might be pushing you toward the same decision you would make if the threat was more than verbal.

Suicidal Ideation (in the absence of depression)

This might surprise many people, because we assume if someone takes their own life it must be due to depression. But depression is not a necessary component in a person deciding their life is not worth continuing, especially if such a decision is made impulsively in conjunction with intense emotion, or as the result of a terminal disease diagnosis.

There are some people who would never consider ending their own lives, regardless of how bad their situation might be, while there are others who would consider such an option rather than live through horrendous circumstances or suffer through a long, slow decline. This is often called "Rational Suicide" most often studied in people with terminal illness who choose to end their lives in their own chosen time rather than wait for an illness to take them slowly. But it is not a new concept. Historically, suicide has often been paired with acts of honor. A leader losing a war might choose suicide, or someone who has disgraced their family and their death is the only way to restore honor.

Even today, we often hear suicide discussed in one of two general categories: As a personal choice, or as a sign of mental illness.

Intense emotion can follow a sudden, unexpected and catastrophic life change, such as financial disaster or the unexpected end of a long-term relationship.

Since this is a book about murder, you can probably guess where I'm going with this: Murder/Suicide. In many of these cases both the murder and the suicide are due to sudden rage and impulsivity, meaning rage results in the murder, and the emotionally impulsive reaction to the murder is suicide. Other cases involve "Altruistic" murder (we will cover this in more detail in the chapter on family killers) in which both the murder and suicide are rationalized as a merciful and necessary way to escape a terrible moment or to avoid a perceived terrible future.

Let's back up for a moment to the third big function I mentioned in the frontal lobes: perception of consequence. This function relies heavily on another function: the ability to predict the future. Does this mean you need to be a psychic? No. The only difference between you and a psychic is that a psychic feels like their predictions are at least partially influenced by something external to them. Predicting the future is something your brain is doing all the time. It is creating expectations based on experience and anticipated outcomes in order to create a sense of predictability. That is why the inability to predict an outcome can create caution and/or anxiety.

What does this have to do with suicidal impulse? Suicide can seem like a rational choice if your ability to perceive and predict the future is critically impaired. And like the other things we mentioned, strong emotion, especially strong sudden emotion, can temporarily create this impairment, and sometimes a short window of time is all it takes to make a critical long-term mistake. Like they say in general "Never make long-term decisions during short-term emotions." A wise saying, but the problem is, short-term emotions impair your ability to perceive long-term consequences.

The overall long-winded point I will repeat throughout this book is that murder is not just a thing of criminals and psychopaths. Most murders every year are by people like us, pushed by circumstance and mood to an extreme we did not think we could take.

The mind of a murderer: Neural structure and homicide?

First a very quick and basic description of how and why the physical structure of your brain is changing all the time: Synaptogenesis and pruning.

Any single brain cell (neuron) can grow connections between hundreds, or even thousands of other neurons. For your entire life you will be constantly forming new connections and shedding old ones. *Synaptogenesis* is the process of forming these new connections between neurons (the point where one neuron communicates with another is called the synapse, therefore the name Synaptogenesis). It is triggered by frequent use of specific neural pathways. When you are born, synaptogenesis is in overdrive. Not just building connections faster than at any other time in your life but building many more connections than you will need. That is where *pruning* comes in. As the name implies, pruning is the process of shedding connections that are not being used. This process is going on in your brain all the time. Any single brain cell might have just a handful of connections to other cells, or might have thousands, depending on the function of the cell. Pruning is not a bad thing; without it your brain would be constant chaos and it would be nearly impossible to focus on a single thought. Learning and experience influence both synaptogenesis and pruning throughout your life, meaning the specific neural connections in your brain right now are different than they were a year ago, and they will be different a year from now. Something else that can influence these processes are health and stress. More on that in a moment.

Neuroscientists have long looked for structural differences in the brains of killers. Are there differences? Yes. Most often in the key amygdala and frontal lobe pathways (Sajous-Turner, *et al.*, 2020), but we cannot answer the causal question of whether these differences lead to homicide because these differences are present in many people who never commit crimes. We also cannot assume the individuals were born with these differences unless we have detailed brain imagery taken during childhood.

Can these changes occur throughout the lifespan? Absolutely.

Chronic stress is known to produce the same kind of structural damage to the brain as seen in murderers (Zhang, et al., 2018), as does serious head injury (Allely, et al., 2014). Similar structural differences are seen in many of the personality disorders as well as some cases of Autism Spectrum Disorder (ASD) and Attention Deficit/Hyperactivity Disorder (ADHD), yet murder is not higher in these populations than the general population so we cannot point at this alone as being causal.

It is easy, when studying a specific population and looking for common traits in the population, to forget to consider how common those traits might be outside the population. For example, if I study everyone currently on death row in the United States and discover that all of them at some point in their lives ate hamburgers with pickles on them, does that mean hamburgers and pickles are a causal factor? I might make that assumption if I did not consider how common that is in the general population.

Can these structural differences be a piece of the puzzle? Definitely. But we walk into a jungle of structural differences causing behavioral dysfunction, therefore entering the realm of mental illness, therefore coming back to the same problem of mental illness more often resulting in harm to self rather than harm to others. We head into that lane in the next chapter.

Chapter Four
Mental Illness and Murder

Each year, mental illness accounts for less than 15% of all murders. People with severe mental illness are much more likely to harm themselves, or be harmed by others, than to harm others. But because we feel murder requires the presence of a mental illness, we dive deep looking for any history of mental health issues or treatment in murderers. Any history, no matter how minor or distant, is immediately assumed to be a contributing factor.

Why is such an assumption so appealing? Because it is an easy answer and makes people feel safer. It is frightening to think that "normal" people can be driven to kill. If you believe it is more likely to be people with a mental illness, then you can feel more confident that you could spot them and avoid them. As you can imagine, this assumption is terrible for the mental health community. The feeling, in general, that people with mental health issues are inherently more dangerous can lead to them being ostracized by community, friends, and family. This is a tough chapter to do because simply by writing about it I risk reinforcing many of these stereotypes. Keep in mind throughout the chapter, this population represents a statistically small threat; much smaller than the "neurotypical" general population.

The belief that people with severe mental illnesses are more dangerous is a circular, self-supporting belief. Meaning, if you believe they are more dangerous, then anyone who is dangerous must, by definition, be mentally ill. It would be like claiming only Chevrolets are involved in accidents, and if you show me a different brand of car in an accident, I insist it must be a Chevrolet because all accidents involve Chevrolets. I might cling to this belief from the emotional need to feel safe from accidents in my Honda. Keep in mind, even though this chapter is about Chevrolets and accidents, the other brands combined are in far more accidents.

Prior to the 1990s, the reported percentage of murderers with severe mental illness was much higher (Richard-Devantoy, Olie, &

Gourevitch, 2009). As the murder rate began to decline in the mid-1990s, the percentage of murders by people with severe mental illness began to drop. What happened? It would be nice to say it was the result of improved treatment and community care, which is partially true, but it was mostly methodology. Through most of the twentieth century the mental health community held the same stereotypes as much of the general public: If you murder someone, you must be mentally ill. Therefore, with no preexisting mental health issues or diagnosis, a person would be diagnosed post-hoc based on the fact they had committed a murder. That was the only symptom. No previous mental health issues, but arrested for murder? Instant diagnosis of Antisocial Personality Disorder, Borderline Personality Disorder, or Schizophrenia, among others. Stereotypes artificially create the environments that support the stereotypes.

Before addressing specific categories I will mention additional factors that are present in most of the cases of people with severe mental illness who commit murder:

- They are not currently receiving treatment and/or are not on medication that could stabilize behavior.
- They lack support from the environment, either the medical community or family.
- There is a current substance abuse problem.

In other words, mental health alone is usually not the only problem.

My apologies in advance to workers within the mental health industry and people familiar with the Diagnostic and Statistical Manual of Mental Disorders (American Psychiatric Association [APA], 2013) who will notice that I seem to be separating substance-related disorders from the category of mental illness in an attempt to avoid stereotyping disorders in general, while at the same time running the risk of stereotyping substance use disorders specifically. Substance-related and Addictive Disorders suffer the stereotype of not being genuine mental illnesses (people will say the use of a substance is a choice, but experiencing psychosis is not), but because of that they are also not victim of the same stereotypes applied to other disorders. Let's establish first why substance use disorders, which originate in the choice to first use the substance, can transform into a disorder. We go back to the functions of the frontal lobes and their role in impulse control and decision making. Why do people reach a point where choosing to stop is a difficult or impossible choice? Because the part of your brain needed to fight the impulse is itself being impaired by the substance and the survival instinct which drives survival-related behavior moves the substance of abuse into the category of "needed for survival" at the same level as food and water.

Why am I separating them for the sake of example in this chapter? For a reason mentioned earlier, when someone commits a murder, we will look for any mental health issue in their history to validate the assumption that only people with mental health issues commit murder. But more importantly, specific to the subject of this chapter, substance use disorders are most problematic when combined with any of the other DSM-5 disorders we are going to cover.

I am not going to go down the list of all mental disorders, because most have no connection to homicide; we will cover the few which top the list: Disorders in the Schizophrenia spectrum, and the mood disorders (Bi-polar and Major Depressive Disorder) which account for the majority of murders where mental illness is considered a primary factor. I will also address a growing stereotype that Autism Spectrum Disorder puts a person at risk for homicidal behavior (this has escalated due to a handful of mass shooters who were on the spectrum, and post-hoc diagnosis of several serial killers). Autism-spectrum is statistically insignificant as a homicide risk, but I will cover a couple high-profile cases which fueled the stereotype. As I mentioned at the beginning of the chapter, only 15% of murders each year are associated with mental illness Ten percent of murders are connected to untreated schizophrenia or bi-polar disorder.

The Schizophrenia Spectrum:

It was long suspected that schizophrenia was not a single disorder, but multiple disorders which all shared similar observable symptoms. Empirical evidence for this started to grow in 2014 when a study by Arnedo and associates (2014) identified at least eight different genetic markers associated with schizophrenia. This made sense because of the variety of symptoms and onset in cases, from severe cases that emerge early in life and have poor prognosis for recovery, to cases which appear later in life triggered by chronic stress and traumatic experiences and have better recovery outcomes. Advances in medication have made it possible for some people diagnosed with schizophrenia to live virtually symptom-free (except for side-effects of the medication) whereas fifty years ago they would not have been able to function.

Even before the empirical evidence began to emerge, the DSM-5 in 2013 recognized the variation when it introduced the schizophrenia spectrum which included the previous categories of schizophrenia and added Schizotypal Personality Disorder and Schizoaffective Disorder (a mood disorder) under the umbrella of schizophrenia. There used to be several identified subtypes of schizophrenia, such as paranoid, disorganized, etc., but research demonstrated frequent overlap of symptoms, so although these are still recognized as symptoms, they are no longer considered unique subtypes. For example, what used to be called Paranoid Schizophrenia fits more accurately under the umbrellas of either delusional disorder, or "schizophrenia with paranoia" than it does as its own label.

A diagnosis of schizophrenia requires at least two symptoms present a significant amount of time for at least a month. At least one of the symptoms needs to be delusions, hallucinations, or disorganized speech (representing disorganized thinking). The other two categories are grossly disorganized or catatonic behavior and negative symptoms (negative meaning the absence of typical function, usually meaning diminished emotional expression or problems initiating goal-directed behavior).

People with schizophrenia are far more likely to hurt themselves, or be victimized by others, than they are to harm other people. The violent stereotype is perpetuated by media because when a person with a serious mental illness harms someone it tends to get more media attention (therefore seems more common) than the same crime committed by someone without a mental illness.

Aggression in schizophrenia is rare, but is more common in younger males, especially when there is a history of aggressive behavior, non-adherence with treatment, impulsivity, and especially substance use and abuse (American Psychiatric Association, 2013).

I mentioned earlier that modern treatments and medications allow many people to live functional lives, whereas decades ago their symptoms would have been too severe. There is good and bad to this, the good is obvious: Fewer hospitalizations. The bad is refusal to follow clinical advice or to take medication. There are obvious ethical concerns around forcing people against their will to take medication. Why would someone refuse medication if it helps them to be functional? Usually because at first the uncomfortable side-effects (such as tremors, sleepiness, dizziness, etc.) are better than symptoms of psychosis. But once the medication causes the psychotic symptoms to recede, the side-effects feel more prominent and become more bothersome. It is easy to start thinking "I'm doing fine now; the side effects are the problem," and be tempted to wean off the medication, allowing the symptoms to gradually creep back. If the problem had been delusional disorder, one of the first cognitions to creep back in can be a feeling of "finally being clear-headed" and the belief that the medication was an attempt at mind-control, or worse, an attempt to harm.

Medical pessimism and suspicion in the person's social support network, especially family, can also lead to refusal of medication and cancelling treatment.

Probably the most gruesome example of this was Richard Chase, who killed at least six people during a serial-killing spree in 1977 and 1978. He was nicknamed "The Vampire of Sacramento" because he would drink the victim's blood and would sometimes eat parts of their organs.

Chase displayed signs of delusional beliefs and aggressive behavior in childhood and as an adult was placed under in-patient psychiatric care twice in the years before the killings. In 1976 he was involuntarily committed after injecting himself with rabbits' blood. He believed he needed blood from animals or people in order to survive. His blood obsession was his primary observed symptom. After several months of treatment with psychotropic drugs his symptoms receded, and he was able to function normally. He was released to his mother's care at her request under the condition that she monitor him (meaning he should live with her) and make sure he took his medication. He was initially doing fine under her care and on the medication, but his mother decided he did not need the medication, and living with her was making him dependent, so she weaned him off the medication and got him his own apartment with roommates to monitor him. Unfortunately, the bizarre behavior returned, Chase returned to a pattern of drug use (including LSD, which you can imagine is not a good choice for someone with a history of schizophrenia) causing the roommates to eventually move out and leave Chase alone in the apartment. That is when the killing started.

A cautionary tale because he likely would have been fine (and his victims still alive today) if the advice of medical professionals had been followed. We will see a similar scenario later when we detail the case of Andrea Yates.

Keep in mind, to a person experiencing delusions, the delusions feel like "truth" and the side-effects of medication feel like an attempt by outside forces to manipulate and control. It's not hard to see why this fuels the motivation to resist the medication.

In January 2020, Australian podiatrist Paul Leslie Quirk killed his wife and dog thinking they were demons who needed to be banished from the earth. He had gone through a decade of cycling between being functional while on medication and experiencing dangerous delusions when going off medication. He had again gone off his medication in the weeks prior to killing his wife.

Also in 2020, Eltiona Skana, a 30-year-old woman with a history of paranoia, delusional beliefs and aggression when not medicated, stopped taking her medication and a month later killed 7-year-old Emily Jones in a park in Bolton, England.

You can probably see both sides of the ethical dilemma. Personal rights to accept or refuse medical treatment, versus risk to public safety.

Bi-polar disorder:

In 1996, as part of the "America Undercover" series, HBO aired a documentary titled "Back from Madness: The Struggle for Sanity" which followed four people in treatment for mental illnesses:

schizophrenia, major depressive disorder, obsessive-compulsive disorder, and bi-polar disorder (then still called Manic Depressive Disorder). The individual with bi-polar was functional while on medication but was frequently hospitalized and often arrested when off his medication. At the end of the documentary he is once again off his medication, behaving very erratically, and living a life of homelessness. In reference to being off medication, he says "at least I am free!" I would argue that although he feels free, he is not. His condition prevents him from having the cognitive clarity to make true free-will choices. He is living at the whim of a biochemical imbalance which might feel good to him but is creating nothing but problems.

For the sake of being technically correct, Major Depressive Disorder is called "Unipolar Depression" because of the "polar" spectrum between mania and depression it involves only depression. When major depressive episodes alternate with either manic or hypomanic episodes it moves between the two "poles" therefore is "bi-polar depression" or simply bi-polar. Bi-polar Disorder is separated into bi-polar I and bi-polar II, the difference being manic episodes in bi-polar I and hypomanic episodes in bi-polar II. What is the difference between manic and hypomanic? Duration and intensity. Both are defined in the DSM-5 (APA, 2013) as "A distinct period of abnormally and persistently elevated, expansive, or irritable mood and abnormally and persistently increased goal-directed activity or energy." In Bi-polar I this must be present for at least a week while in bi-polar II it lasts at least four days. The symptoms must be present most of the time every day during that span of time.

We need to pause here to clear up some confusion when interpreting DSM 5 criteria. There are two primary symptoms which individually, or together, need to be present regardless of the other symptoms to qualify as a disorder: Symptoms must cause the individual subjective distress and/or impair important areas of functioning (such as work or social functioning). If it does not meet these criteria, then the symptoms are merely traits, they do not represent a disorder. In the case of bi-polar disorders, manic or hypomanic symptoms must impair functioning, but subjective distress is not a requirement. Can you guess why? Because manic and hypomanic episodes can feel good and be very productive, even if the behavior is being destructive to self or others.

The other mistake when interpreting bi-polar disorder is assuming manic always means feeling good or happy, and depression always means feeling sad. That is often true, but manic and hypomanic mean high-energy states, like having the gas pedal to the floor all the time, while depression is a low energy state where it can be hard to initiate anything and sometimes even organizing thoughts can feel like an exhausting task. In other words, in a manic or hypomanic state, any emotion the person is experiencing, good or bad, is being experienced in an elevated high-energy way and will result in an exaggerated outward display. If they are happy, they are *very* happy (such as laughing at things which are not funny, or laughing excessively), if they are angry, they are suddenly very angry. If they get sad, they experience a high energy exaggerated sadness which can result in sudden tears and impulsive self-destructive behavior. On the flip side, in major depressive disorder an individual is sometimes so low in energy they do not have the energy to be actively self-destructive.

Do you see where in the bi-polar criteria the potential for impulsive murder might lie? I mentioned earlier that any strong emotion can impair the frontal lobe functions of impulse-control, decision-making, and perception of consequence. In the case of manic episodes these functions are diminished during the entire episode regardless of other factors. Imagine adding to this a sudden burst of anger or the addition of a substance of abuse and you have a person with little or no conscious control lashing out at whatever target is nearby.

On June 24, 2016 Texas mother Christy Sheats called a "family meeting" with her husband (who was supposedly seeking a divorce) and their two daughters, Taylor (age 22) and Madison (age 17). She then started shooting, killing Madison instantly, and injuring Taylor, who ran into the street. Christy followed her, shooting her again, then returned to the house to reload. Police arrived as Christy was shooting Taylor a final time. When she refused to drop the weapon, police shot her to death. Taylor later died at the hospital. Christy did not shoot her husband, who later stated she likely killed their daughters to make him suffer. In the chapter on filicide (parents killing their own children) I will mention Sheats again as a statistically rare subcategory of filicide.

This case combines both momentary rage and mental illness. Sheats began to spiral in 2012 when both her mother and grandfather died within months of each other. The gun she later used to kill her daughters had been a gift from her grandfather. After 2012 she was hospitalized several times after suicide attempts, and police had been called to the home on several occasions due to spontaneous and impulsive self-harming incidents thought to be suicide attempts. Media reported Sheats as having been treated for depression and anxiety, but the impulsive nature of her self-harming could easily fit within manic or hypomanic episodes of bi-polar disorder.

This incident gained national attention from gun control groups because Christy was a vocal supporter of gun rights, having posted on her Facebook page the accusation that Democrats were trying to take away her guns and prevent her from being able to protect her family. No surprise that the irony of her beliefs versus her actions would attract attention. And with a history of mental health treatment she easily fit and reinforced the stereotype of mental illness being dangerous to others.

I want to emphasize, however, that most commonly when these conditions are met, the target is the self, not another person. In bi-polar disorders self-harm is just as likely in the manic or hypomanic states as in the major depressive state because of the high energy that comes with it. If you look through lists of known celebrities with bi-polar disorder it will be obvious that self-harm is far more common than harming others (Author Ernest Hemingway, singer Scott Weiland of the Stone Temple Pilots among many others). Singer and Actor Frank Sinatra was bi-polar (at that time called Manic Depression). Anthony Summers and Robbyn Swan in their Sinatra biography "Sinatra: The Life" (2005) quoted Sinatra as saying "Being an 18-karat manic depressive, and having lived a life of violent emotional contradictions, I have an over-acute capacity for sadness as well as elation."

Major Depressive Disorder:

As you can imagine, of the three disorders we have covered, this one is far more likely to involve harm to self than to anyone else. When Major Depressive Disorder does lead to murder it involves one of two main motivations: Revenge (Murder/Suicide, "If I'm going out, I'm taking you with me"), or Altruism (perceiving that a loved one will experience long-term personal or environmental suffering due to the suicide "You will be better off coming with me").

Before we detail those two motivations, we must return to the brain, and by no surprise, the frontal lobes. We use the term "Depression" here in two ways, one as a low mood, the other as low neural energy. Remember the example in bi-polar as manic being the gas-pedal to the floor, the brain running very fast creating an intense and exaggerated experience of whatever emotion is being experienced. Depression is the opposite. The brain physically runs slower, processing speed is reduced, and the important frontal-lobe functions of impulse-control, decision-making, and perception of consequence struggle to do their jobs. What other function is in the frontal lobes? The motor cortex, which sends motor commands for movement, and pre-motor areas which initiate movement. In very deep bouts of depression it can be physically hard to move, and even the effort to think can be difficult, let alone the ability to focus on anything remotely complex. In addition to impairing perception of consequence, depression also impairs the ability to think about future events, especially the ability to imagine your own future. Think about the stereotypical question "Where do you see yourself in five years?" We answer that question by projecting our current goals into the future. In depression it can be difficult, if not impossible, to feel any sense of a future self. It's not a premonition that life is over, although it can produce that feeling, it's an impairment in something called "Episodic Future Memory:" Our ability to predict our own future and imagine ourselves in that future. If you are planning to go out tonight you can picture yourself doing it before it happens, if you are planning a vacation in a couple months you can mentally visualize yourself on that vacation (part of how we judge an event as good or bad depends on how closely it meets our expectations when we imagine it beforehand). It might seem silly to call something "memory" when it has not happened yet, but it gets that label because in Anterograde Amnesia, where you lose the ability to form new memories, you also lose the ability to project yourself into the future, which means the function is connected in some way to memory processing. This is the dark lure of depression; the slowing of neural activity can subjectively feel like a sense of clarity, and the brain will give preference to memories which fit the depressed mood (an effect called "Mood Dependent Memory" or "Mood Congruent Memory" in which the brain more easily cues up memories similar to your current mood). You feel like there is no future because your brain will not allow you to visualize the future, and you think everything has always been bad because your brain silences, restricts, or diminishes any positive memories or thoughts. Subjectively, it feels like you are "finally seeing the truth," and the way you feel right now is how it will always be. The truth is your brain is lying to you to preserve and magnify the depressed mood. Hopefully you can understand why it is a pit difficult to escape once you have started down, and the cognitive restrictions and inability to see ahead is why the saying "suicide is a long-term solution to a short-term problem," is accurate.

Just as these factors prevent the depressed person from seeing a future beyond what is happening right now, it can also prevent them from seeing a future for dependents, such as children or a partner. A person considering suicide could believe it is a gift to take loved ones too, saving them from future misery. The key factor is whether the individual sees themselves as someone the others depend on (they will suffer without me), versus seeing themselves as a burden to them (they will be better off without me). Whether the loved ones will truly suffer long term does not matter, the person in the grips of suicidal ideation cannot accurately see a future beyond what they are experiencing right now.

Suicidal ideation can exist for a very long time, sometimes years, without ever leading to an attempt on one's life. But its presence is a risk factor. You might be in a situation now when sometimes, when things are going particularly bad, the thought crosses your mind, or you spend an extended time contemplating it, but it passes. You might have loved ones who are dependent on you for their well-being or survival and you believe you would never ever cross that line. You might believe that if things got bad enough that you would consider taking your own life, but you would never take theirs. Cognition can change rapidly as you take the darker steps toward attempting to end your own life. If you have moments of suicidal ideation, it is a gift for both yourself and your loved ones to speak to someone. Reach out for support. Don't take the chance. Yes, it is easier said than done, and the depressive state itself makes the effort seem impossible. Which is why suicide hot lines exist as an easier first step. In the United States the national suicide hotline is: 1-800-273-8255, and as of July 2022 simply dialing 988 can connect people to the network. It can be accessed via call, text, or chat. Nearly 100 countries have set up some form of crisis hotlines.

Does the brain completely surrender to these extremes? Does it ever try to pull us back from the edge? Yes. But often after the damage is already done. In response to a destructive action the brain sometimes delivers a true "moment of clarity" likely related to our survival instinct. This can be as simple as instant regret when you have said something hurtful, or more intense regret if you have physically hurt someone (not to be confused with people who intend to hurt someone and have no regret afterward).

In 1995 Jason Scheiber was riding his motorcycle down a steep street when he hit a 6-year-old girl riding her bike in the street. She was dragged 75 feet and died. Scheiber was so distraught he laid down in the grass, pulled a pistol from his jacket, and shot himself in the head (APnews, 1995). Obviously, this was not a murder, but it demonstrates the extreme reaction that can come when your actions have unintentionally caused a death.

It is unknown how many murder/suicides involving partners might result from the same kind of scenario; an angry physical outburst, unintentional death, shifting the angry emotional energy immediately to regret, but with the same high-powered irrational emotional intensity that was fueling the rage. In these types of cases neither murder, nor suicide were intended, they escalated from out-of-control emotions.

Another form of regret can be directed at the self. For example, when a person in the depths of depression and suicidal ideation has taken an action that could result in their death, the survival instinct will frequently kick-in, giving them a true "moment of clarity," realizing the reality and magnitude of what they are doing. In such cases the person is likely to call for help. Does this mean people who make a serious attempt (an act that could cause death if not interrupted by medical care) and survive are less likely to do it again later? Yes. Less than ten percent of people who attempt a suicide requiring hospitalization later die from another attempt (Owens, 2002).

TRIGGER WARNING: If you have lost someone to suicide, skip this paragraph. Ken Baldwin, who is now a speaker and suicide-prevention advocate, is a perfect example of the moment of clarity. In the summer of 1985, he attempted suicide by jumping from the Golden Gate Bridge in San Francisco. He is one of only a couple dozen people to ever survive the jump, and all the survivor's stories are similar. No matter how dark their mindset, no matter how certain they were that death was the answer, no matter how much they thought they wanted it, the instant they let go of the bridge they regretted it. The veil was pulled back and all those thoughts that were being held back or blocked by the depression were free. As Ken said, "everything in my life that I'd thought was unfixable was totally fixable - except for having just jumped" (Taylor, 2011). We can never know the experiences of the jumpers who did not survive, but we can assume from the accounts of survivors that regret is probably more common than we realize. You can see why it is often advised to get guns out of the environment of people who are considered a high suicide risk. A gun gives no time for regret. By forcing them to use a slower method, there is a chance the regret can kick in and they can be saved. This is also a factor in why men have more completed suicide attempts even though women attempt suicide more often; men tend to pick guns. A greater chance of being immediately lethal, and no time for regret.

A long-winded trip around the block to set the cognitive stage around depression, but let's get back to the two primary categories of murder when the killer intends suicide: Revenge, and altruism.

Revenge:

When we look at mass shooters and school shooters, we will find this is a common theme. Suicidal intent and revenge fantasies. It is also a very common cognition in people who never kill anyone. "If I'm going out, I'm taking someone with me."

Given that most revenge murder/suicides are by men it will come as no surprise that men more frequently experience revenge fantasies (Goldner, Lev-Wiesel, & Simon, 2019). If your experience suggests women are more likely to have revenge fantasies, it is likely because women talk about theirs more, while men are more likely to practice silent rumination. Talking out negative emotions is a better path to reducing them than silently ruminating over them.

In a nutshell, a revenge-based murder/suicide with only two victims comes from the same cognitions as those that produce a mass shooter, the only difference is whether the revenge target is a single person, a small group, or an entire demographic.

Altruism:

As I mentioned earlier, this comes from the belief that someone you leave behind will suffer due to your death, so taking them out with you is perceived as an altruistic act to save them from suffering. These are most common when a primary caregiver, who is the sole financial support for the family, is experiencing a financial catastrophe. The greatest risk factor in these cases is in the individual keeping the financial problems hidden from the rest of the family. Like revenge fantasies, silent rumination is more dangerous and deadly than seeking support from family and friends. Social support is a powerful tool, and there is no shame in asking for help.

Risk factors (many of these overlap):

- A male with traditional gender role expectations of being primary family support.
- A single parent of any gender with limited or no social support.
- History of mental health problems.
- Sudden career loss with no immediate employment prospects and primary responsibility to support dependents.
- Living paycheck-to-paycheck in a financially uncertain

profession.

- Any of these combined with hiding the problem from family.
- Any of these combined with a substance of abuse.

Autism Spectrum Disorder

This has entered the conversation in the last decade because of Seung-Hui Cho (Virginia Tech in 2007), Adam Lanza (Sandy Hook Elementary in 2012), Elliot Rodger (mass shooting in Santa Barbara in 2014), Nikolas Cruz (Marjory Stoneman Douglas High School in 2018), and the post-hoc diagnosis of Jeffrey Dahmer as being on the autism spectrum even though he was never diagnosed with it while he was alive.

Unlike the other disorders I covered in this chapter, there is no statistically significant link between autism spectrum and murder. What creates the assumption of a connection is the high profile cases I just mentioned, and the tendency for people on the lower functioning end of the autism spectrum to have "meltdowns" that can sometimes result in hurting people (but like other disorders, is more likely to result in self harm).

I commit a full chapter later to mass shooters and school shooters, but I will cover both Lanza and Rodger here because specific traits of autism spectrum were contributors to their actions. They are also good examples of something we will see throughout the book: An uninterrupted progression toward the behavior, which could have been interrupted at several points during development.

On the morning of December 14, 2012, **Adam Lanza** shot his mother to death, then drove to Sandy Hook elementary school. At 9:35 a.m. he shot his way through a glass panel next to the locked front doors of the school; entered the school, and began a shooting spree lasting only five minutes, resulting in the deaths of 20 students, 6 staff members, and finally himself. The first officers arriving on the scene reportedly heard Lanza's final shot.

Because Lanza took his own life and the life of his mother, initial reports and investigation were little more than speculation; it took time to piece together the influences that likely led to the shootings.

Lanza was identified early in life as autism-spectrum, and initially received accurate diagnosis and support. Later he also developed Obsessive-Compulsive Disorder (OCD) and was suspected of suffering from anorexia nervosa because his weight at autopsy was 112 pounds; far below the norm for a person 6 feet tall.

A more likely reason for his low weight, given his environment in the last months before the shooting, is lack of self-care, and his mother withdrawing from interest in providing care.

Lanza had attended Sandy Hook elementary for a little over four years, but he began to have problems functioning in school, and when he started middle school, he found the format of moving between rooms to attend each class, requiring walking through crowded and noisy hallways to be stressful and anxiety provoking. In the second year of middle school he was moved to "homebound" status. At this point his primary symptoms were problems with communication, specifically interpersonal communication, and sensitivity to stimuli such as noise and external activity. He returned to school for his freshman year in high school, earning a spot on the honor roll, but again had problems with social interaction and overstimulation, and by the next year he rarely attended school, and finished high school being homeschooled.

At this point there was nothing outside the norm for Lanza considering his position on the autism spectrum. Definitely nothing that would point toward violent behavior.

Investigations into his medical history found he was receiving frequent evaluation and help until 2006, and his parents seemed very involved in helping him. What happened after 2006? There was growing conflict in the parents' marriage, finally ending in divorce in 2009. Adam's father had visitation rights, but the two had very little interaction. Adam's older brother Ryan by this time was out of the home attending college. Adam's mother had gone from a family situation where there were others to offer support, to having sole responsibility for Adam. By multiple accounts, the two became more and more distant, until in the end Adam was practically bound to his room, communicating with his mother almost exclusively through email, refusing contact from his father, and eight months before the shootings cut off all communication with his older brother. His room was his entire world, his primary comfort zone, and through the internet he was growing more and more obsessed with mass shootings in general, and school shootings specifically. Because no one was closely monitoring him, this obsession was able to progress with no interruption.

The final straw was his mother's intent to sell the house and move. She planned to ease the blow by gradually transitioning Adam into an RV before selling the house, but the idea of losing the familiar and comfortable space of his room was not simply stressful, it was from his perspective the end of his world.

And here is where I must step into a politicized mess which will make some of you immediately defensive and angry. Adam Lanza did not have the functional abilities necessary, nor the independent financial resources, to seek out and purchase weapons on his own. He would not have been able to carry out the shooting if the necessary weapons were not present in his home. He might have still acted out violently and attacked his mother, possibly still killing her with other weapons in the environment, such as knives or blunt objects, but he would not have been able to kill 26 people in five minutes. A knife would not have got him through the locked doors at the school, and even if he gained entry, a person armed with a near-proximity weapon like a knife, club, anything else that requires close proximity to the victim, is easier to overpower and apprehend.

In a nutshell, Lanza went into an uninterrupted three-year spiral which ended because his environment gave him everything he needed to play out his growing obsession. His autism traits did not create the spiral, they simply served to accelerate it. Problems of social communication and social interaction were to be expected, but his isolation from his immediate support system, his family, was a red flag that went on for months without being addressed.

Another case that drew public attention to autism occurred just two years later. On the evening of May 23, 2014, 22-year-old **Elliot Rodger** killed his two roommates and one visitor as they returned to their shared apartment in Isla Vista, California, near the University of

California at Santa Barbara (UCSB). He then drove to a coffee shop, purchased a coffee, and from his laptop in his car posted a "Retribution" video to YouTube in which he described his intent to carry out a mass shooting, and mailed a lengthy manifesto titled "My Twisted World: The Story of Elliot Rodger" to over thirty people including his therapist and parents. He then drove to the Alpha Phi sorority house near UCSB with the intent of carrying out a mass shooting within the house. Strangely, instead of forcing his way in, he knocked on the door several times and waited for someone to answer. When there was no answer, he started shooting at anyone nearby, then got in his car, randomly shooting at people and ramming pedestrians. His spree lasted only fifteen minutes, but in that time he killed six people and injured fourteen. After being injured exchanging gunfire with police, Rodger was found dead in his vehicle with a self-inflicted gunshot to the head.

Whereas Lanza's primary problems were isolation from his support network and increasing obsession with school shootings, Rodger's primary problems were persistent deficits in social communication and social interaction leading to repeated failures in attempting to develop social relationships, specifically with women. In the end, Rodger was the textbook definition of "Incel," an "involuntary celibate" who is unsuccessful in forming relationships with women, perceive women almost exclusively as objects for sex, and feel they somehow deserve or are entitled to sex from women. Rather than recognizing their own role in their failures, they place all the blame on women; forming deep hostility toward women, and envious hatred toward sexually successful men. They are frustrated or angered when they see others in relationships (referred to as "Chads and Stacys"). It is not hard to imagine how someone who sees themselves as a deserving partner and blames rejection on women, will be angered when they see women accepting other men. Because incel groups are based on externalized anger toward others, it is no surprise their anger will target almost all demographics, fueling and reinforcing misogyny and racism.

Elliot Rodger became a role model for Incels, inspiring at least six other incel-fueled attacks over the following eight years. Among them, Alek Minassian, responsible for the "Toronto van attack" in

April 2018, which killed 11 and injured 15, who declared on Facebook prior to the attack "The Incel Rebellion has already begun! We will overthrow all the Chads and Stacys! All hail the Supreme Gentleman Elliot Rodger!" (Bacon, 2018).

Rodger himself had no such role models or precedent for his attacks, so what led him down that path? We must start early and look once again at a progression of anger allowed to build without interruption despite warning signs. And unfortunately, a failure of authorities to respond when late warning signs were brought to their attention.

Rodger was born in London, but his family moved to Los Angeles when he was five years old. His father, Peter Rodger, was a London filmmaker who moved the family in order to work in Hollywood (he was an assistant director on "The Hunger Games" in 2012). This is important because Elliot was not raised directly within Hollywood social culture, but he orbited the culture, seeing enough of it firsthand that it had an influence on his early socialization and social expectations (he was seen appearing with his father at movie premieres, award shows, and other Hollywood red carpet events).

Elliot displayed developmental issues early, entering therapy when he was eight years old, but it was not until he was 16 that he received a formal diagnosis of Autism Spectrum Disorder. By comparison to Adam Lanza, Elliot Rodger was on a higher functioning end of the spectrum, able to maintain enrollment in school and attend regular classes. The primary symptoms which caused him problems in school were deficits in social communication and social interaction, which led to being perceived as peculiar, not understanding how to initiate or respond to social interactions. This caused him to be the frequent target of teasing, sometimes escalating to bullying. As is often the case, this resulted in Rodger sometimes lashing out at others when he sensed being rejected or ridiculed. He later claimed he had trouble making friendships, but those around him said he tended to push people away when they attempted to befriend him.

This resulted in a pattern which does not require the presence of Autism at all and is far too familiar to women in the United States. When Rodger would attempt to flirt with women and be rejected, he would lash out and be hostile toward them.

Here is where the Hollywood environment makes this worse. But first we need to back up to Adam Lanza again. Adam was the more severe end of the spectrum, which means he was emotionally cemented to routine and familiarity. If you have ever worked with children on the more severe end of the spectrum you know it can be difficult getting them to accept a new person or shift to a new task or routine. This was a major point in Lanza feeling his life was over when hearing his mother was going to sell the house and he was going to lose his one comfortable space: his bedroom.

Rodger was not that severe, but as you work your way toward the higher functioning end of the spectrum there are still echoes of that attachment to routine. Higher functioning people can have a very rigid view of the world and a nearly unbending set of opinions. Their early childhood socialization, including social norms, gender norms, and social and gender expectations attached to those norms can be difficult, if not impossible to change. Their view of the world is very black and white with little room for nuance or variation.

Rodger's expectations of social interaction were formed by observing the most shallow and superficial of social interaction environments: Hollywood. Where from an outside perspective it looks like any attractive man simply has to show interest or snap his fingers and women will be swooning. Where people pair-up by status rather than romance. Where sexualization is on display more than personality, and the nuance of working into a relationship is often not visible. Because the public often does not see the day to day interactions and gradual build-up into a relationship, it can appear relationships form very quickly.

In other words, Rodger did not understand the "social dance" of two people getting together and gradually forming a relationship. It seemed to him to be as simple as "Hey, you're hot, let's hook up" and sex would follow. In his manifesto he did not talk about the lack of an emotional or romantic relationship, only about the lack of sexual relationships. His interest in women was driven by a desire for sex, not for emotional intimacy or companionship. This is what made him the definition of "Incel" and a later role model for that population.

By the time he was 18 his parents were divorced, and his father was in a new marriage. His parents, independently, continued to offer help and provide resources for therapy, but he rejected most attempts to help and became more isolated and increasingly hostile toward women and couples. According to his manifesto he threw coffee on a couple because he was jealous of them and would sometimes splash coffee on women who would not smile at him. He resented women for rejecting him, and men for being romantically successful when he was not. He attended college but considered it primarily a place where it should be easy to hook up and have sex. Two years before the shootings he started thinking about violence toward the people who were rejecting him. He started purchasing weapons and went to firing ranges to practice.

Much like Adam Lanza, Elliot Rodger spent the next two years spiraling. Becoming more hostile and obsessed with violent fantasies of revenge and retribution to those who had rejected him. His parents took a distant approach, offering financial assistance and therapy, but little if any direct engagement.

His YouTube videos became more direct and alarming in their anger and implied violence, and in April 2014, just weeks before the shootings, his parents notified local police who contacted Rodger but determined there was not sufficient evidence for involuntary mental health commitment. It was an unfortunate decision because California law would have allowed for emergency psychiatric evaluation (involuntary) in this case if only the officers had done a background check to identify recent gun purchases and viewed the YouTube videos that had caused the parents concern. Months after the attack California added a "red flag" law which, in addition to allowing police at the time to detain Rodger, would have allowed them to temporarily take away his weapons until he was determined to not be a threat to himself or others.

In his final video, released on the evening of the attacks, he says "You girls have never been attracted to me. I don't know why you girls aren't attracted to me, but I will punish you all for it ... I don't know what you don't see in me. I'm the perfect guy and yet you throw yourselves at these obnoxious men instead of me, the supreme gentleman."

Obviously, police missed an opportunity to either stop or delay his actions weeks before the shooting, but is there a way to better identify mass shooters before they carry out the act? The age of social media is providing better clues and a possible solution in identification; we will cover that later in the chapter on mass shooters.

In a nutshell, Adam Lanza and Elliot Rodger had traits associated with autism spectrum disorder which helped fuel their progression, but nothing in their progression was unique to autism (such progression also occurs in the absence of autism), and as we will see in the chapter on serial killers, the diagnosis of Jeffrey Dahmer was a post-hoc diagnosis after his capture which was shoe-horned in as an attempt to explain his behavior.

Of the disorders covered in this chapter, autism-spectrum has the lowest statistical probability of leading to homicide. Again, I covered it because of public perception, not because of any statistically significant connection or theat.

Next, we will look at the different categories and motivations of filicide: When parents kill their own children.

Chapter Five

Killing Family Members

On July 20, 2001, shortly after her husband left for work, Andrea Yates prepared breakfast for her five children, then starting with her youngest child, six-month old Mary, took them one-by-one into the bathroom where she had filled the tub with nine inches of water, held them face-down in the water, and drowned them. When the last child, seven-year-old Noah, saw what was happening, he tried to run. She chased him down, dragged him into the bathroom, and drowned him as well. She then called 9-1-1 with an erratic and incoherent plea to send police, then called her husband and told him to come home. Police found Noah's body still in the tub with his youngest sibling lying on him, and the three others laid in their beds.

She immediately confessed to the killings, saying she was doing it to save them.

Andrea Yates falls into the category of Altruistic Filicide: Killing your own children out of love or for their benefit. How can ending their lives in such a nightmarish fashion be love? What was motivating her to think she was doing something good for her children? We will get to that in a moment.

Phillip J Resnick has studied filicide since the late 1960s and has determined five primary categories of filicide (Resnick, 1969) along with subcategories within each (Resnick, 2016).

- Altruistic filicide
    - o Filicide associated with suicide.
    - o Filicide to relieve or prevent suffering.
- Acutely psychotic filicide
- Unwanted child filicide
- Child maltreatment filicide
- Spouse revenge filicide

We will address each of those, starting with the case of Andrea Yates and why she fits altruistic filicide, to relieve or prevent suffering, but possibly crosses over both subcategories.

The case of Yates is tragic in many ways, obviously the loss of the children and the method of their murder, but in how preventable it was. The mental health system did everything within its legal limits to prevent the outcome, but people cannot ethically or legally be forced to follow the recommendations.

In many of the examples I use in this book the motivation to kill can be traced to environmental or mental stressors relatively recent to the act, but in the case of Andrea Yates it was a long, slow progression of internal vulnerabilities combined with environmental stressors.

Andrea Yates was born in Hallsville, Texas in 1964. In 1982 she graduated from Milby High School in Houston as class valedictorian and captain of the swim team, but also suffered from bulimia, depression, and according to at least one high school friend, had occasional suicidal thoughts. She went to school to study nursing and worked as a registered nurse from 1986 to 1994. In 1989 she met Russel Yates, a fellow tenant in the apartment complex where she was living. They moved in together shortly thereafter and were married in April 1993. According to Russell, they planned to have "as many babies as nature allowed," (Kumari, 2019) but it is unknown if Andrea equally shared this vision. Their first child, Noah, was born in February 1994. Soon after, Russell accepted a job offer in Florida requiring Andrea to quit her nursing job. They lived in a trailer in Seminole Florida, but the job did not last long, and they moved back to Houston and lived in a motor home. By the time they had their fourth child they were living in a renovated Greyhound bus (Spencer, 2015). It was after the birth of the fourth child, Luke, that Andrea showed signs of depression, including two suicide attempts, that within a month escalated to postpartum psychosis and led to hospitalization. Russell moved them out of the bus and into a small house (for the sake of her health). Her psychiatrist at the time strongly advised them to not have more children, as the episodes would most certainly repeat, and perhaps get worse, but just seven weeks after her release from the hospital Russell encouraged her to stop taking the prescribed medication, so it would not interfere with another pregnancy. A short time later they conceived their fifth child, Mary, who was born in November 2000. Andrea went back on medication and by most accounts seemed to be doing well until her father died the following March. After that she stopped taking medication, began self-mutilating, and required immediate hospitalization. She was treated and released, but a month later became nearly catatonic and filled a bathtub with water in the middle of the day in what doctors later assumed was an intended suicide attempt (Yates herself admitted later she had intended to drown the children that day). She was immediately hospitalized again.

If doctors considered her a high suicide risk, she should have stayed hospitalized until she was no longer a threat to herself, but this is where the story becomes very frustrating for those of us involved in the mental health profession who can see when family is helping in the process versus harming the process. This is where Russell Yates harmed the process. The doctors did everything they could within their legal rights, but when Russell wanted Andrea released from the hospital the doctors had no legal ability to stop him. The best they could do, which they did, was advise him to never leave her alone. There needed to be someone with her all the time. This is the advice Russell chose to dismiss, and as soon as he left her alone, she killed her children.

Those are the surface details of the case, but it still does not explain the cognitions which led Andrea to her final act or why I place her in the category of altruistic filicide. Let's rewind and go into her head and look at the influences that were nudging her toward that cliff.

Who was Andrea on the day she met Russell Yates? She had been class valedictorian, an officer in the National Honor Society, captain of the swim team, had completed a pre-nursing program at the University of Houston and graduated from the University of Texas Health Science Center at Houston. She was working as a registered nurse, independent and self-supporting. There was nothing about her indicating she sought a marriage of traditional gender roles: Husband as King and wife as passive and subservient whose primary responsibility was bearing and raising children. When Russell later said they would "have as many children as God allowed," was he speaking for her as well? Or was that what Russell wanted? Russell came from a religiously conservative upbringing with very strict gender roles; it is not hard to understand why that would become his expectation for his own family. Andrea did not come from the same kind of environment.

There is another character in this plot, a "traveling preacher" named Michael Woroniecki who had been known to visit college campuses handing out pamphlets attempting to scare followers his direction by telling people they were going to hell. Russell Yates was attending Auburn when he first encountered Woroniecki and they kept in contact for several years afterward. The converted bus the Yate's later lived in was purchased from Woroniecki. Many who follow the case believe Woroniecki influenced Andrea directly, making her feel like a failure as a mother; planting the seed that because of her failings her children were condemned, but it is just as likely Russell embraced these ideas from Woroniecki's pamphlets and used the threat of the children's salvation to keep Andrea in line.

Imagine a person with a history of depression, who was academically gifted and motivated, who had been independent and self-supporting, finding herself within a single year leaving Texas for Florida, quitting her job and becoming financially dependent on her new husband, going from a house to a trailer, and selling almost all the possessions she had acquired over the years to downsize into a limited environment while having her first child, and the following year having a second child. According to Andrea's long-time friend Deborah Holmes, Russell put all child-care responsibility on Andrea, and as the children got older also put all home-schooling responsibility on her. Russell insisted on selling possessions when they moved so "the children will not become materialistic," but Russell did not sell his own possessions; he moved them into a storage unit.

She was hospitalized following a suicide attempt after the birth of their fourth child. This was likely the culmination of growing depression, not a sudden isolated event, and it was from this point forward Russell seemed to interpret Andrea's emotional struggles as a personal weakness to be overcome rather than a mental health issue to be treated. On several occasions Andrea very likely could have been saved with extended in-patient treatment, but Russell needed her taking care of the children, and despite childbirth being a trigger, it did not stop him from wanting even more children. Russell seemed to turn toward biblical solutions more than medical solutions, and it was here that the seed of "bad mother equals condemned children" took root and Andrea's depression started feeding the idea that it was impossible for her to be the kind of mother who could raise "saved" children; condemnation was the children's destiny. Eternal salvation could only come if she took their lives before it was too late.

And here is where Andrea Yates' act is one of altruistic filicide. From her perspective she killed her children to save them; to protect them from eternal damnation. Any momentary terror or suffering they might experience would be immediately rewarded by salvation. It was a better fate than eternal suffering. She was giving them the ultimate motherly gift.

In the earlier bullet point I mentioned two sub-types of altruistic filicide, to prevent suffering, and filicide associated with suicide, which is related: The parent intends to take their own life, and to save their children the pain of losing a parent and whatever perceived horrors might await them afterward, the parent takes the lives of the children as well. Andrea is also a fit for this subset because she intended "death by institution" meaning she expected to receive the death penalty for what she had done. She was not an active suicide, but she intended her own death as well as the deaths of her children.

Andrea is also a hit in almost every risk category for mothers who commit filicide: Married with high levels of stress, lack of support from spouse, primary caregiver of multiple children, not employed, social isolation and limited social support. When first married, Russell took Andrea away from her family and her job, and forced her to sell her possessions, he made her completely financially and socially dependent on him and took away almost all physical reminders of her previous independence. After her final hospitalization, when she was not to be left alone, Russell brought in his mother to spend time with her, but felt Andrea was getting lazy and needed a "kick in the pants" to get her back to being a responsible mother. Over the course of years, he provided an environment guaranteed to destroy her.

If you are interested in diving deeper into this case, I would suggest the book "Breaking Point" by Suzy Spencer, which does a good job filling in the details, history, and surrounding environment.

In filicide associated with suicide, mothers will take their lives and the lives of their children, but fathers are more likely to kill the entire family, including the mother. Is this because men are more homicidal and controlling by nature? Possibly. But the easier answers are the socialized gender role expectations programmed into men from a very early age. They are told they are the protectors and providers. The survival of the entire family sits on their shoulders, therefore if they are collapsing or failing, the entire family will suffer. It is not hard to see why suicidal ideation in a father carries the risk of perceiving disaster for the entire family, therefore ending their lives can also be perceived as altruistic; a way to save them from whatever terrible life awaits them afterward.

There is an important point to make. It is not that the children or family will truly have a terrible life after the parent is gone, it is that the parent perceives they will. Sometimes it can be as simple as imagining the family suffering just from hearing the news of the loss of the loved one. Keep in mind, depression strips away the ability to realistically imagine the future. This leads to a feeling of foreshortened future, as if part of you realizes there is no future for you, and naturally you might extend this lack of a future to your loved ones as well, therefore it can seem very rational that ending their lives along with yours is "saving" them.

Another common victim category of altruistic filicide to prevent suffering or end current suffering are children with disabilities. These can occur at any age; frequently motivated by the parent's perception of the child's quality of life and the magnitude of daily care required by the parent. The greater the disability, the higher the risk.

In 2014, Tania Clarence of New Malden, England, suffocated her three youngest children in their beds shortly after her husband and oldest daughter had left to visit relatives in South Africa. All three children had spinal muscular atrophy type 2, condition that requires nearly constant care. She was reportedly "overwhelmed" by the care requirement and the realization her children would not have long lives (BBC, 2015).

I need to emphasize a point here. The risk is not lessened in a two-parent household if one parent still has primary caretaking responsibility. The greater the social support, and the more that support duties are shared, the less the risk.

Acutely psychotic filicide is self-explanatory. Killing children or family members as the result of a severe episode resulting from mental illness. In such cases the person is not fully aware of their actions or the consequences of their actions, and the victims are a matter of proximity in the moment rather than being targeted specifically because they are family.

Dena Schlosser of Plano Texas was experiencing a psychotic episode when she felt God was instructing her to cut off the arms of her baby with a kitchen knife. Like Andrea Yates, her husband was involved in a fundamentalist church which felt mental illness was a sign of demonic interference and needed prayer rather than medication or professional treatment. In a surprising coincidence, she was placed in the same psychiatric facility as Andrea Yates, and they reportedly became friends.

Unwanted child filicide. Most often associated with mothers who do not bond with the unborn child during pregnancy, this can also be caused by the child potentially causing severe financial, emotional, or social distress. These are the cases you hear about in the news of newborns being found in dumpsters, or public restrooms, or being dropped off elsewhere. This is unfortunately so common it has resulted in establishing "Safe Haven" laws and drop-off locations where newborns can be dropped off without harm to the baby or legal repercussion to the mother.

Unwanted child filicide can be as passive as abandoning the child knowing it will die from exposure, or as direct as intentionally killing the child and disposing of the body.

The cases at highest risk are pregnancies resulting from sexual coercion or assault, as those are cases where the child is most likely to become emotionally associated with the assailant and enduring the pregnancy itself can feel like a private continuation of the assault, and cases where the mother would have preferred to terminate the pregnancy but was prevented due to social, economic, or environmental pressures. More generally, any situation which reduces or prevents emotional bonding between child and mother (such as postpartum depression) can increase the risk.

In 1994, Susan Smith, a South Carolina mother of two strapped her two children (ages 3 years and 14 months) into their car seats, then rolled her car into a lake, killing both children. She claims she did it because she was having an affair with a man who did not want children.

Statistically, most cases of unwanted child filicide are newborn or recently born infants, but older children can be victims as well. Often the children are "tolerated" for several years before a triggering event drives the parent to kill them to have them out of the way. This is different from maltreatment filicide which we will cover next.

Child maltreatment filicide is the result of either severe neglect or abuse leading to death. Of the categories of filicide, this is the one where the death was not an intended outcome, but rather a consequence of the parent's actions (or lack of action). Munchausen's by proxy (clinically Factitious Disorder Imposed on Another) would fall within this category. That is when a parent will either falsify medical symptoms in a child or do something intentional to cause symptoms in order to receive medical or social attention or sympathy.

In 2015, Lacey Spears was found guilty of killing her 5-year-old son with poison after repeatedly sickening him in order to chronicle his "chronic illnesses" in an online "mommy blog" and on Facebook.

Spousal Revenge Filicide is the rarest of the filicide categories, a parent killing a child to exact revenge on the other parent.

What drives people to these extremes? Underlying mental illness is often present, but not necessary. As in the case with almost every category of murder throughout this book, momentary irrational rage, in which perception of long-term consequence is briefly disabled in the brain, can lead people to murdering anyone, including family.

In May 2001 Mary Jean Pearle dropped off her two daughters Faith (age 8) and Liberty (age 6) for an scheduled dinner at the mall with her estranged husband John Battaglia. Instead of dinner at the mall he took the girls back to his apartment, called Mary and made her listen as he shot both girls to death.

Earlier I mentioned Christy Sheats, the Texas mother who in 2016 killed her two daughters in front of her husband, while sparing him, supposedly to make him suffer. If this account is accurate it is a textbook example of spousal revenge filicide.

These cases are very dramatic and get a lot of media attention, but as I mentioned, they are the rarest of filicide cases.

Let's close filicide with a case which crosses several of our definitions. On November 9, 1971, 46-year-old John List, who lived with his family in a 19-room mansion in Westfield New Jersey, shot his mother and wife, then shot two of his children as they returned home from school. He made himself lunch, then drove to the bank to close his and his mother's bank accounts. He then went to the high school to watch his son's soccer game. Upon returning home he shot his son, removed all photos of himself from the house, and left a confessional letter for his pastor claiming he saw too much evil in the world, so he had killed his family to save their souls. He sent letters to the children's schools and jobs saying they would be visiting an ill relative for a couple weeks, and stopped all milk, mail, and newspaper deliveries. Because the family was known to be reclusive, no one entered the house to discover the bodies for nearly a month. Meanwhile, he left his car at Kennedy airport in New York as a lure before taking a train west, eventually ending up in Colorado where he assumed a new identity and got an accounting job. He eventually remarried. He was not discovered until May 1989 when the program "America's Most Wanted" covered the crime, including a well-done age-progression of List which was recognized by one of his Colorado neighbors.

List's claim in the letter to his pastor makes this appear to be a case of altruistic family annihilation not simply filicide. Most commonly in cases of family annihilation the perpetrator ends it with taking their own life, but List never intended to take his own life. He planned his exit carefully and made sure (by removing pictures of himself) it would be difficult to find him.

John list came from a very typical family for his time. Strongly embedded gender norms of the father as provider and protector, with self-identity and self-worth being strongly connected to those expectations. List had joined the military immediately out of high school in 1943 and while serving overseas his father died. List later claimed to suffer PTSD from his experiences during the war, and if true, the loss of his father while overseas would have compounded this.

Given the financial troubles later described by List, the purchase of the mansion in Westfield stretched their resources and was likely an attempt to display an image of wealth they did not have. In 1971 the bank where List worked closed and he was laid off. Here is where we have a genuine red flag: Because the idea of father being respected as provider and protector was such a large part of his identity, he hid his unemployment from the family. He continued to dress everyday and "leave for work," where he would linger at the train station scouring the newspapers for another job. Having access to his mother's bank account, he started funneling money from her account to continue paying the mortgage on the house. He could not bring himself to do anything that would reveal the urgency of their financial situation to the family.

As I mentioned, there is no indication that suicide was ever in his plans; years after his conviction he said in an interview he did not consider suicide because it would have kept him from going to heaven, where he hoped to be reunited with his family. But given his plan to move to another state and get a new job, why not simply take the family along? He could not bring himself to consider any option that would expose his failures: Losing his job and not being able to provide for the family.

In typical cases of murder/suicide or family annihilation due to circumstances like this, the main motivation is the perceived impact on the family. The perception that they will struggle or suffer due to the financial collapse, and therefore ending their lives is merciful. In the case of List, however, the primary driver seemed to be ego: How others would perceive him in a negative way. It was not their suffering he was trying to avoid; it was his own humiliation. This would put him in the realm of "unwanted family." He needed to relocate to find a new job, and he needed the family gone because they were an expense he needed to cut, and a humiliation he could not endure.

List was sentenced to five consecutive life terms. He died in prison on March 21, 2008 from pneumonia at the age of 82. If not for his appearance on America's Most Wanted it is very likely he would have never been found.

We have covered parents killing their children; it's time to flip to the other side of this coin:

Parricide, when children kill their parents. More specifically, Matricide when killing the mother, and Patricide when killing the father. Parricide is relatively rare, less than two percent of murders each year (Heide, 2013), but it gets a lot of media attention; especially when it is either shocking or tragically petty, such as Daniel Petric, the 17-year-old who in October 2007 killed his mother and wounded his father because they would not let him play Halo 3.

It is popular for people to point at parricide cases as an example that the current generation is somehow more violent or dangerous than previous generations, but parricide has always been with us, and in our lifetimes, especially in the United States, the rates have changed very little. The only difference today is the amount of attention the cases receive through mass media and social media.

The most recognizable historical case is probably Lizzie Borden ("Lizzie Bordon took an axe and gave her mother forty whacks, when she saw what she had done, she gave her father forty one") who in 1892 was accused of killing her father and stepmother by hacking them up (she was ultimately acquitted because the evidence was all circumstantial, but the court of public opinion was certain she was guilty).

Research usually separates parricide motivation into three categories: Severely abused, mentally ill, or dangerously antisocial.

Dangerously antisocial parricide is connected to killing the parent because they represent an obstacle to a goal, or their death will bring a desired reward (such as inheritance or life insurance payout).

In August 1989, Lyle and Erik Menendez shot and killed their wealthy parents. After initially claiming they came home from a day out to discover their parents dead, they later confessed to the killings, saying they had experienced years of abuse at the hands of both parents, and on the day of the killings feared for their own lives. The prosecution insisted the brothers were after the parent's money; noting the brother's lavish spending in the six months between the killings and their arrest. The brothers were initially given separate trials, both resulting in deadlocked juries. Upon retrial the brothers were tried together and ultimately found guilty of first-degree murder.

If the brothers are telling the truth, they are in the "abuse" category of motivation; if the prosecution is correct, they are in the dangerously antisocial category. Is trying to cover up the crime and then later living the high-life as big spenders evidence the killings were not motivated by abuse? No. An abuse victim might attempt a cover-up (such as claiming someone else did it) if they know the abuse has been hidden and would be difficult to prove, and the rapid spending of the parents' assets is both revenge and celebration of being free of the abuser. Neither brother chose to live in the family mansion afterward, each purchased their own condo. This could be seen as wanting to avoid the memory of the murder, but it can also be seen as avoiding a place associated with years of traumatic memories.

Mass shooters and school shooters can cross any of these categories. If an intended mass/school shooter lives with a parent, they will frequently start their spree by killing them before moving on to their intended targets. This can be motivated by abuse or mental illness but can also be perceived by the killer as altruistic: Saving the parent from having to witness the aftermath of what the shooter intends to do.

Intimate partner violence. Killing those we love most. It is sometimes said that love and hate are opposite ends of the emotional spectrum. That is not true. Love and hate share a residence on the same end of the spectrum; apathy is the opposite end. That is why love can turn to hatred so quickly and with such intensity.

By no surprise there are big gender differences in this category. When women kill male partners, outside of mental illness, it is most often due to either jealousy, or self-defense in a domestic violence situation. Women rarely engage in murder-suicide when killing an intimate partner. Males will kill partners for altruistic rationale (the same reasons for killing the entire family), or out of jealous rage, or unintentionally during an act of severe physical abuse. Men are much more likely to engage in murder-suicide when killing an intimate partner. There are between 1,000 and 1,500 murder-suicides each year, and of those between 65% and 75% involve intimate partners. Of those, 95% involve women killed by a male partner (Violence Policy

Center, 2020). The risk for women is even higher during pregnancy.

Let's step inside the cognition that leads to murder in a relationship. You can already imagine a very common one: When facing a break-up, the partner on the receiving end of the break-up might have the thought "If I can't have you, no one can." You might think this is an exclusively narcissistic trait, but, like most domestic abusers, it is rooted in deep-set insecurity creating a need for control to prevent the partner from leaving. Therefore, when the partner does leave, there is a sense of lack of control, not just of the relationship, but of the abusers' life in general. It is common for an abuser to feel powerless in their day-to-day life, such as at work, and counter the insecurity by being overly controlling at home with family.

Another common cognition is an altruistic one. The partner is facing a disaster of some kind, financial collapse or serious legal trouble, and has decided to end their own life. They can have the perception, just as parents can have with children in cases of filicide, that they are "saving" the partner from the pain and struggle of being without them. Again, it does not matter if the perception is realistic, only that the offending partner feels it is true.

Domestic violence homicide is also extremely dangerous for others in the immediate environment. According to the Violence Policy Center (2020) up to 20% of total victims in murder-suicide domestic homicides are family, friends, or law enforcement who are also present. Over the last forty years, domestic disturbance calls account for up to 30% of law enforcement deaths each year, more than any other type of police call.

We have bounced around the issue, but what makes a relationship turn from love to violence so quickly? Obviously in the cases of altruistic murder-suicide it is the depth of love that creates the perception the victim is being given a gift. But what about situations involving rage and jealousy?

Unlike any other relationship, one with an anticipated life-long intimate partner is one where you trust another person with your emotional vulnerabilities and intend to share the rest of your life journey with them. There is an expectation they will always be there for you, they will share all the big future events, they are built-in support for all the challenges ahead. You will never face anything alone. There is a lot of emotional intensity which comes with that kind of bond. When that person does something that violates that trust and takes away the stability of your future, it is not hard to see how the intensity of the bond with them can turn from positive to negative very quickly. It is a high-revving engine which suddenly shifts into reverse.

On the flip side is a relationship in which a partner is viewed as a servant, or at worst, a possession to be owned and commanded with the expectation of unswerving obedience. These are relationships rooted in insecurity and an intense need for control, sometimes the result of a mental health issue, but often rooted in childhood abuse. Not only is there no trust, but fear and suspicion of betrayal are always bubbling under the surface, ready to erupt. This type of person desperately needs a sense of control because at some point in their life they were traumatized by lack of control, so when a partner tries to leave, or defies the control in some way, there can be a very rapid and very intense response of emotional instability and rage in which the controller feels like *they* are the victim of control and potential abuse by the other partner and they rationalize that their aggressive or violent response is a legitimate and necessary defensive response. The behavior of the partner is perceived as threat, and in a very real way it triggers the fight/flight response to use aggression to stop the threat.

Control and possession murders most commonly have one of two cognitive roots, either the "if I can't have you, no one will" mentality which was the assumed motivation in the 1994 murders of Nicole Brown Simpson and her companion Ron Goldman by her ex-husband (actor and former American football star) O.J. Simpson, or unintentional homicide resulting from momentary rage with the intent to hurt but not kill, which was assumed in the 2021 death of Gabby Petito by her boyfriend Brian Laundrie, who then dumped her body, drove cross country back to his parent's home in Florida, and shortly thereafter killed himself in a wilderness area near the home.

Before we talk about the risk factors of harming your partner, and whether you think it is something you could ever do, let's talk briefly about emotional pain.

Some key points about committed long-term relationships:

- They are a biochemical addiction, which causes physical withdrawal when they end. Oxytocin (the love hormone) increases as a couple begins to bond and stays rather consistent afterward. When a partner leaves, oxytocin levels drop, and you feel it, you even crave it, which is why partners sometimes break-up multiple times and keep getting back together, and why we are at risk to "rebound" into another relationship shortly after a break-up. Your body becomes accustomed to a higher base level of the hormone, and when that hormone drops off, it wants it back (Schneidermann, et.al, 2011).

- For some people, losing a partner through divorce can be worse than losing them through death. For the same reasons mentioned previously, plus another big one: When a partner dies, they are still "yours." The bond is still there even though they are physically gone. But when they leave for another relationship, not only do you not have them anymore, but someone else has that bond now. It is loss, betrayal, and rejection all rolled up into one tidy ball of emotional pain.

- The body processes emotional pain in a very similar way to how it processes physical pain. Have you ever seen someone experiencing extreme emotional pain? Their facial expression contorts the same way it does during physical pain, they might double-over or fall down writhing, again just like someone experiencing physical pain. It turns out many of the same areas of the brain which process physical pain also process emotional pain (Eisenberger, 2003; Najib, 2004; Meerwijk, 2013) and send similar motor responses to the body. This is also why it is tempting to cope with emotional pain using the same substances used to reduce physical pain.

Combine all these factors in a single "perfect storm" and you can understand how unexpected betrayal and rejection slams you psychologically, physically, and biochemically. Recipe for disaster. This would hit anyone especially hard but imagine how much worse it could be if it hits someone who is already prone to angry outbursts, aggressive behavior, and/or problems regulating strong emotions.

Do you sometimes "lose control" when you are angry? Do you hit people or throw objects at people when you are angry? It does not mean you are a murderer waiting for a victim, but it means you are at greater risk than others of taking that deadly step if the precipitating factors all hit within a short period of time.

A final word on family killing.

In the opening chapter I mentioned that murder is widely considered the worst crime you can commit, yet also the one we try most to excuse. This is true in family killing as well. Across history and across cultures it has been excused, and even endorsed, under the label of "Honor Killing." It should come as no surprise that globally, and historically, the majority of Honor Killing victims were women and girls because cultures tend to put the most restrictive behavioral norms on them.

Even when the killing of a partner does not fall under the label of Honor Killing, there are still loopholes and excuses placed into the laws, such as the French Penal Code of 1810, where Article 324 gives the husband an excuse for killing his wife: "Murder, committed by the husband, upon his wife, or by the wife, upon her husband, is not excusable, if the life of the husband or wife, who has committed such murder, has not been put in peril, at the very moment when the murder has taken place. Nevertheless, in the case of adultery, provide for by article 336, murder committed upon the wife as well as upon her accomplice, at the moment when the husband shall have caught them in the act, in the house where the husband and wife dwell, is excusable."

The concept of a "crime of passion" or a crime caused by a sudden and uncontrollable surge of emotion, specifically rage, became a common legal defense in many countries and did not start to receive serious challenge until the 1970s. In a back-door way it has also been used to reinforce the social expectation of public modesty in women because "men can't control themselves," therefore sexual harassment or assault was at least partially blamed on the victim "leading on" the assailant.

Three specific verses in the Bible have been viewed historically as endorsing honor killing:

- "'If a priest's daughter defiles herself by becoming a prostitute, she disgraces her father; she must be burned in the fire" [Leviticus 21:9]

- "Anyone who curses his father or mother must be put to death." [Exodus 21:17]
- For God said, 'Honor your father and mother' and 'Anyone who curses his father or mother must be put to death.' [Matthew 15:4]

Obviously over time public attitude and cultural norms change, and with them the laws change as well. For example, we no longer stone people to death for gathering wood on the Sabbath [Numbers 15:32-36].

Historically, family annihilation was frequently excused if the family had dishonored the father or the broader family, or if the father could no longer support the family. The ancient Hindu tradition of Sati expected a widow to throw herself upon her husbands' funeral pyre and burn to death with his body.

Again, we consider killing to be a terrible crime, but frequently make excuses for it, not only for criminal reasons, but often for reinforcing cultural traditions and norms.

Chapter Six

Healthcare Killers

Healthcare killers fall within three primary motivations:

- **Heroes**: Intentionally cause medical emergencies so they can save the person, but sometimes fail.

- **Psychotic**: Motivated by a homicidal impulse who use the umbrella of the medical industry to provide victims and hide their actions.

- **Altruistic**: Perceive they are saving victims from prolonged suffering and a long, slow death.

All of these would technically be labeled "serial killers" because of the number of victims separated over time, but we will save that technicality for the last chapter.

Let's start with some of the basic tactics predators and manipulators will use to attract victims while also avoiding detection. Predators will seek out a profession, or group identity, which will give them access to victims, while at the same time the group identity makes it less likely they will be suspected, and more likely accusers will be doubted. Especially by those who hold the same group identity. We are hardwired to be social creatures, to identity with a group as part of our survival instinct. A byproduct of that is the tendency to feel that an accusation against someone in the group is an accusation against an important part of our identity and we will instinctively defend, dismiss, or justify the behavior.

Fire Departments will deny or diminish the frequency of fire-bugs being attracted to the firefighting profession, but in the 1990's the FBI's Behavior Analysis Unit (BAU) had collected enough case studies to put together a profile for Firefighter Arsonists (Homeland Security, 2003). Due to the large number of volunteer firefighters in the United States, with lesser requirements or certifications for the job, it is easy for an arsonist to enter the profession and use it as cover for setting fires. These people tend to be the "hero" category: Setting fires so they can respond to them and heroically extinguish them.

Even trained, career firefighters can use the job to hide their crimes. Most famously, John Orr was a chief arson investigator with the Glendale, California Fire Department, and a prolific arsonist, eventually convicted of four deaths which occurred during a fire he started at a home center store. He was suspected of setting at least eight fires over three years.

Sexual misconduct allegations against youth pastors are in the news so frequently, that for some people the term "youth pastor" immediately conjures suspicions of predatory behavior shrouded under the group identity of Christian innocence.

Con artists trying to get money out of groups will learn the language and behavior of the group and echo it, convincing people they are part of that group, because we are more trusting of people if we share a group identity with them. Serial killer Dennis Rader, the BTK killer, (Bind, Torture, Kill) was a Church and boy scout leader. This made it less likely anyone would suspect the "good Christian man" of being a monster.

As political division has increased in the United States there has been an increase in con-artists targeting both extremes of the political spectrum to raise money for causes unique to the political fringes.

In all these cases it's not that the targeted groups are bad, it's that bad people will seek them out as shelter. It makes it worse when the organizations will try to cover up these instances to protect their image. This has been a historical problem with both churches and the health care industry.

It is not hard to understand why people with a homicidal impulse, or a medical hero complex, would be attracted to the medical field. Easy access to vulnerable victims, and an environment in which deaths are likely to be attributed to existing illnesses or injury.

"Heroes:"

In the late 1970's and early 1980's **Genene Jones** worked as a licensed vocational nurse at two hospitals in Texas and was later suspected of killing up to 50 infants and children under her care in pediatric units. Her first employer, Bexar County Hospital near San Antonio, noticed a statistically unlikely number of infant deaths in the pediatric intensive care unit and suspected someone in the staff was likely responsible. Rather than risk public acknowledgement by trying to identify and prosecute the guilty person, they laid off the entire staff of licensed vocational nurses in the unit and replaced them with registered nurses. Afterward, the mortality rate dropped.

Jones moved on to a pediatrician's clinic in nearby Kerrville, Texas. When children started to die at this clinic as well a doctor was able to identify Jones as the cause. She was originally convicted on only two cases which would have led to her release in 2018. In 2017 prosecutors charged her with several other cases and she eventually received a life sentence. During the process of seeking additional charges, prosecutors discovered that Bexar County Hospital had destroyed all records which could have been used to convict her of deaths at that facility (Texas Public Radio, 2017).

Jones falls into the "hero" category because she would inject the infants and children with drugs, cause a medical emergency, then rush in to miraculously save them. Unfortunately, she frequently failed.

It was rumored that she had worked at more than those two facilities, but upon her arrest, other facilities destroyed all documentation of her employment in order to avoid harming their public image and to avoid the possibility of legal liability.

Kristen Gilbert (Strickland) was born and raised in Fall River Massachusetts, a community along the Massachusetts border with Rhode Island, less than 20 miles from Providence. It is a community that peaked in 1920 with a population of over 120,000 and has been shrinking ever since (down to 94,000 in the 2020 census). Other than Kristen, Fall River is better known as the birthplace of George Stephanopoulos, Emeril Lagasse, and Lizzie Borden (the house where Lizzie grew up and killed her parents is now a bread and breakfast).

Kristen's father was an executive, her mother was a homemaker and part-time teacher. Kristen was the oldest of two daughters. By her teen years Kristen had a reputation for frequent lying, making violent threats to people who angered her, and faking suicide attempts for attention and to manipulate people. After high school she initially attended Bridgewater State College (now Bridgewater University), but after another staged suicide attempt, she was placed briefly in psychiatric treatment. Afterward she briefly attended a community college before transferring a final time to Greenfield Community College where she studied nursing and in 1988 became a registered nurse. She quickly secured a job at the Veterans Affairs Medical Center in Northampton Massachusetts where she worked from 1989 until 1996.

Just a couple years into the job she was considered a responsible and capable nurse who was quick to respond when patients experienced sudden medical emergencies. Her coworkers became suspicious, however, when they noticed there were more deaths and "medical emergencies" when she was on duty. For several years no one pressed the issue or initiated an investigation until 1995 when inconsistencies in medical supplies led to evidence that she was intentionally causing medical emergencies so she could heroically respond to them. An investigation was started, during which Kristen phoned in a bomb threat to the facility to try to derail investigators. She left the job due to the investigations. Over the course of several months she checked herself into psychiatric hospitals no less than seven times, never staying more than ten days. By the time of her arrest she was suspected in multiple murders during her career, having been on duty during half of the 350 patient deaths which occurred at the facility during her time there. She was only charged with the last four which occurred after she was already under suspicion.

Kristen is another case of someone using medication to intentionally cause a medical emergency so she could step in to help save them. Another motivation might have been her boyfriend, who worked security at the hospital. Security was required to be present during medical emergencies. She might have sought to impress him with her heroic performance. Such attention-seeking behavior would fit the mold of someone who would put others at risk in order to be in the spotlight while attempting to save them.

You might already be wondering, is there a disorder that is likely common among healthcare killers who are seeking attention or praise through the hero role? Yes. A disorder mentioned in the previous chapter: Factitious Disorder Imposed on Another, previously known as Factitious Disorder by Proxy, or by its more recognizable name, Munchausen's by Proxy. In which someone will cause harm to another for the attention it draws to them or to manipulate others to perceive them in a positive and/or sympathetic way. This is different than Malingering, in which there is an obvious external reward being pursued by the deception, such as money, medications, or avoiding liability for an action.

I need to emphasize that it takes a trained clinician directly observing and interviewing the individual to make a diagnosis of any disorder, we cannot diagnose simply from what we hear or see in media. No matter how much a publicized behavior might seem to fit the criteria for a diagnosis, there are always differential diagnoses (more or equally likely possibilities) which can only be pinpointed through direct evaluation. Factitious Disorder is often comorbid with Borderline Personality Disorder, but not always, so we cannot make that assumption. Kristen Gilbert is often assumed, due to past behavior, of having Antisocial Personality Disorder, Borderline Personality Disorder, or Histrionic Personality Disorder, but she was never formally evaluated for those or formally diagnosed with any of them.

The error many "armchair analysts" make (and a mistake many people being trained as clinicians need to learn not to make), is to focus on the primary criteria for a disorder and selectively pick out behaviors which fit it while ignoring behaviors which do not, while at the same time ignoring "associated features" (other symptoms which are commonly present but not part of the primary diagnostic criteria). For example, Antisocial Personality Disorder and Borderline Personality Disorder have different primary criteria, but when you combine the primary criteria and associated features of both you find tremendous overlap between the two. In fact, the gender difference between the two (women more likely to be diagnosed Borderline while men are more likely to be diagnosed Antisocial) along with the commonality of symptoms across the two (Chun, et al., 2017) has caused some to wonder if the two are the same disorder with differences in primary symptoms based on gender due to unrealistic gender expectations and socialization. For example, men are socialized in a way which allows (and expects) outward expressions of anger and frustration, while women are socialized to keep "masculine" emotions such as anger internalized, therefore while men are more likely to lash out externally, women are more likely to lash out internally. In other words, when the disorder is present, gender socialization dictates how it will be expressed. Women with Borderline can be aggressive and show disregard for rules or the rights of others (as in Antisocial) but it is not part of the primary criteria, and men with Antisocial can also have irrational fear of abandonment and a pattern of unstable relationships, but again, it is not part of the primary criteria.

A lot of words there to simply say "let's be careful" when assuming disorders based on specific behaviors when we do not have access to the full spectrum of an individual's behavior.

Psychotic killers:

This is the realm of healthcare killers whose primary motivation and goal seems to be murder. And to address the diagnostic cautions I just mentioned, in most cases these people were formally diagnosed, but there are a frightening few who raise the question "How many people who do not fit the criteria for a disorder, would kill a stranger if the opportunity presented itself and there was no consequence?" I cannot present a solid answer to that one.

Charles Cullen spent a collective 16 years working as a nurse between 1986 and his eventual arrest in 2003. He had 29 confirmed victims, confessed to up to 40 victims, but his inability to remember specifics around many of the cases has caused reasonable suspicion that murder became so frequent for him that only certain special cases stand out in his memory and others just blended together as unremarkable or typical. Several times he claimed to have "blacked out" the memories of many of his murders. He could be responsible for up to 400 murders. He attempted to claim his murders were altruistic; ending patient's suffering or saving them from the dehumanizing treatment of the medical field, including attempts to resuscitate patients in cardiac arrest. But many of his victims were not terminal, several were well on the way to recovery and some were close to being released from the hospital.

Cullen was less than a year old when his father died. The

youngest of eight children he claimed to have been bullied by his siblings, their friends, and kids in school. When he was nine years old, he intentionally drank chemicals from a chemical set in what is thought to be the first of many suicide attempts. Suicidal ideation and occasional suicide attempts would recur throughout his life, especially after difficult experiences, usually meaning facing consequences for something he had done wrong. For example, in 1993 he began stalking a co-worker, going so far as to break into her home. He was arrested, pled guilty to trespassing, and received one year of probation. The day after his arrest he attempted suicide, and over the following several months was in and out of psychiatric facilities for treatment of depression after further suicide attempts.

Let's roll back to the previous section. Could this mean the suicide attempts were a form of manipulation rather than a true desire to end his life? We cannot know for sure, but it is a possibility to keep in mind. Given his use of lethal medications to kill others, it is surprising he never used the same medications to end his own life if death was what he truly wanted.

Cullen is another unfortunate example of hospitals and medical facilities avoiding liability and potential lawsuits by letting staff go if they are suspected of harming or killing patients rather than reporting the person to law enforcement, and the lack of a reporting system medical facilities could access when hiring. Cullen worked at no less than seven hospitals and clinics during his 16 years, and even when facilities had evidence or strong suspicions that he was harming people they would simply let him leave. At one facility he was given a choice of being fired or quitting and given a "neutral evaluation" for his next employer. He chose to quit. When trying to determine how many people Cullen had killed, investigators were frustrated to find many facilities had destroyed all records connected to Cullen and his access to patients he could have harmed. It was his last employer, Somerset Medical Center in Somerville, New Jersey, that made the connection between Cullen and patient deaths and alerted authorities. Fortunately, the publicity around his arrest and trial led to new laws and regulations which allowed greater tracking of "problem employees," but unfortunately did not alleviate the problem of medical facilities failing to report in the first place.

During Cullen's years as a nurse, facilities were most likely to monitor drug inventories of substances which were associated with recreational abuse. Inventory anomalies for drugs used exclusively within the facility did not raise the same red flags. Cullen's most common drugs for inducing fatal overdose were insulin (which could cause a fatal drop in blood sugar resulting in coma and death), digoxin, and epinephrine (both of which can cause cardiac arrhythmias leading to death). Again, given his frequent suicide attempts, including one in which he lit a charcoal barbeque in his bathroom expecting to die from carbon monoxide poisoning (his neighbors smelled smoke and called authorities) he had easy access to the means to end his life. And after his arrest he reached a plea agreement with authorities to identify other victims so long as they did not seek the death penalty.

He was sentenced to eleven consecutive life sentences. He will be eligible for parole in the year 2403.

Let me address a question you might have about Cullen, and most healthcare killers in general; do they ever murder people outside a hospital? Usually not. And this is where the label "serial killer" fits them best. They are attracted to a victim demographic, in this case vulnerable people in hospitals, and they stick with that demographic. People in hospitals are "safe" victims because they cannot go anywhere, depending on their condition and prognosis their death is less likely to draw suspicion, and the mechanism of death (drugs) are available on site. They enter the workplace carrying no evidence, and they leave carrying no evidence.

Some have wondered if there was a connection between his own tentative desire for death and the taking of other lives. Was it a way to vent a desire to be around death without personally dying? Perhaps. There might have been some connection there because it seems his killing would frequently pause after one of his suicide attempts. One of his statements after his arrest was that he often fantasized about stealing drugs from the hospital and using them on himself. As we mentioned earlier, why didn't he?

We need to take a brief sidestep into a dark reality about human nature and our survival instinct. We are designed to kill others if survival requires it and designed to resist killing ourselves. As I mentioned earlier, once someone in a deep suicidal depression finally engages in an act that could end their life, the survival instinct often makes one final attempt to kick in and stop it. We do not find any similar instinctual drive preventing us from killing others. It is the rational thinking of our frontal lobes that stops us (or tries to if they are functioning properly) when a homicidal impulse is present. Violence draws us. Think about sex and violence in movies and on television. Over time there have been citizen groups trying to reduce each, but much more energy has gone into trying to limit sex than trying to limit violence. The infamous "Hays Code" which restricted content in movies starting in the 1930s had many more rules limiting the display or implication of intimate contact (limiting the length of a kiss, requiring couples to be shown in separate beds, no images of pregnant people or talk of how babies were made, at the most extreme it even limited the image of cows being milked) but you could kill as many people as you wanted in a film.

So, it is not unreasonable to speculate that Cullen's murders were a way of killing himself without killing himself. Perhaps each murder came with an impulse to turn the needle on himself instead of his victim, and the warring influences never chose him. At its root, that would put Cullen into the cognitive realm of a repeated murder/suicide, but without ever completing the suicide.

Are you at risk of taking the cognitive "baby steps" that would end in making a choice like this? Let's put another slant on Cullen. We established that he does not fit Altruistic killer despite his claims of trying to prevent people from suffering. But it is not out of the question that he could rationalize that a person in the hospital with a serious medical issue is less valuable as a life than people who are healthy and not in the hospital. He might have gone through a repeated impulse of murder/suicide in which he wanted to take someone out with him and chose people whose lives he felt had little remaining value or time. Perhaps each time he injected a drug his intent was to follow with himself, but he could never follow through with the final act. If you were going to end your life, would you have the desire to take the life of a stranger? Do you have any curiosity of what killing another person is like? If not, you're safe. If so, you might be at risk if all the necessary factors came together at the same time.

It sounds callous to consider people with medical issues to have less value as a life, but even "normal" people tend to do that. Do we apply the same value to homeless people that we apply to others? Poor people in general? People who have committed crimes and served time in prison? The elderly? Have you ever seen the "morality" questions that ask questions such as "You are on an airplane with a young couple, an old couple, a man in a wheelchair, and a child traveling alone. The plane is going down. There are only two parachutes and you get to decide who gets them. If you take one, who gets the other? If you do not take one, which two people get the parachutes?" Answering the question at all requires applying a hierarchy to the value of the lives. It's a question that sets us up for the final section:

Altruistic killers:

Altruistic killers believe they are helping to either end suffering or prevent suffering. A common thread among these people is a history of personally witnessing loss, usually a close family member (most often a parent) who died a long, slow, suffering death, and is either saving individuals from having to suffer that way, or saving family members from having to experience it, or both.

I start with a caveat. There are some who believe there is no such thing as a purely altruistic healthcare killer. It is true that some will claim altruism, such as Charles Cullen, when their list of victims shows he was not truly trying to end misery, but the argument against altruism suggests there is a homicidal, opportunistic impulse to have control over life and death, and the choice of victims is a way to self-justify the impulse by rationalizing an altruistic motive when such a motive is not truly present.

Why are we motivated to believe that an altruistic motivation to protect someone from suffering can be a primary motivation? Two reasons. One, it makes the murderer less frightening and less random. It alleviates fear that if we are hospitalized, we could be victim to such a person. Second, it fits gender-norm assumptions. What do I mean by that? Healthcare killers are unique in the overall population of serial killers because there are more women than men. To assume altruistic motivation fits the gender expectation that women are more empathetic and nurturing, therefore it would make more sense that when they kill in a medical setting, there is empathy and altruism behind it.

Of course, to every argument there is a counterargument. I mentioned earlier that predators are attracted to professions and group identities where they can find victims and where the group identity protects them from suspicion. Given that women today still outnumber men in the nursing profession, it would make sense that women with homicidal impulses would find it easier to enter the nursing profession for the opportunities it presents rather than trying to operate outside the profession.

And note, I'm saying women outnumber men as healthcare killers, not that it is all women, or that there are no men. Due to the gender imbalance historically present in the professions of doctor and nurse, when the killer is a doctor, they are more likely to be male, when the killer is a nurse, they are more likely to be female. But overall, there are more nurses than doctors accused and/or prosecuted for killing people under their care.

Let's start with someone who exists in that grey area around what defines "murder." His motivations were most definitely altruistic, and he was labeled "murderer" by some and "trailblazer" by others. Dr. Death himself:

Jack Kevorkian was a vocal "right to die" advocate who, by his own claim, helped at least 130 people end their own lives between 1990 and 1998. As a point of reference, the first "Death with Dignity" act, establishing procedures and rules for terminally ill people who choose to end their own lives, was enacted in Oregon in 1997. As of 2022 there are 8 states, and the District of Columbia, which have Death with Dignity Acts in place, all of them based on the original Oregon act. Kevorkian is seen as the catalyst who brought the conversation of "right to die" into public consciousness and brought about a gradual change in how people perceived the right to choose their own time and place of death.

Between May 1994 and June 1997 Kevorkian was put on trial

four times for assisting suicides. Three ended in acquittal and one in a mistrial. What helped Kevorkian avoid prosecution was his method; he did not administer the fatal dose, he connected the patient to a mechanism which could deliver a fatal dose (or fatal gas in the case of a machine which delivered carbon monoxide), but it was up to the individual patient to push the button and start the process.

However, in 1998 Kevorkian videotaped himself assisting Thomas Youk, a 52-year-old in the final stages of Lou Gehrig's disease. Youk had signed informed and voluntary consent for the process but was not physically capable of administering his own dose, so Kevorkian directly injected the fatal dose. Kevorkian confidently allowed the video to be aired on national television, and this turned out to be his final case. He was arrested, tried, and convicted of second-degree murder and sentenced to serve up to 25 years. Ultimately, he was released in 2007 for good behavior (and likely because Kevorkian himself was terminally ill with Hepatitis C), having served 8 years of his sentence.

Unlike the Death with Dignity Laws in place today, which require a patient have a terminal illness and have agreement with at least two doctors that they likely have less than 6 months to live (and must be of sound mind to make the choice), Kevorkian was criticized for assisting some people who would not have met that criteria. Some patients experienced chronic pain but were not terminal. Kevorkian expressed a belief that endless suffering, whether terminal or not, should be the guideline of giving an individual the right to choose. Some families argued that their loved ones were simply in the depths of depression, and not of sound mind to make such a choice, others that the chronic pain their loved ones were experiencing could have been treated, and the emotional impact of the pain itself meant they were not of sound mind to make such a choice. All these issues created tremendous public debate and influenced the conversation when it came to establishing guidelines and safeguards for the laws eventually passed in the states. This is why every state after Oregon to pass a Death with Dignity Act has used the Oregon act as a model since it seems to do the best job of covering the bases and offering the greatest safeguards possible.

Kevorkian died on May 18, 2011 from the cumulative effects of

Hepatitis C, liver cancer, kidney problems, and pneumonia. He did not terminate himself prior to his death, nor were any "artificial" attempts made to prolong his life.

An epilogue on the Death with Dignity Act and a frequent criticism of the "less than six months to live," qualification. You will frequently hear people attack that with the claim "there are cases where people were given six months to live and they recovered and lived for thirty years."

No. There are not. There is not a single documented case of someone who was given that six-month timeline and recovered to go on and live a long life. There are cases of people who were told, upon initial diagnosis of a potentially terminal illness, that they had two years or less, and then later went into remission and lived long lives, and there are cases of people given the six-month prognosis who managed to stretch it out to a year or year and a half, but no one has ever fully recovered when their condition places them in that six month window.

Harold Shipman an English General Practitioner who was active between 1977 and 1998 is a difficult one in the altruistic category because he never talked about his motives. Altruism is often assumed because of the age and poor health of his victims (despite poor health sometimes having been entered in medical records by Shipman after their deaths), but also questioned because of valuables he sometimes took from in-home patients after their deaths. His final victim, Kathleen Grundy in 1998 changed her Will giving most her money to Shipman. It was later found to have been falsified by Shipman.

Why do we lean toward altruistic motives, at least at first, with Shipman? Because he is in the category of having witnessed a long, slow death of a relative, in this case his mother who died after a long battle with lung cancer when he was 17. He had been very close to his mother, and the only reprieve from pain he noticed in her during her decline was when doctors gave her injections of morphine. Later, as a doctor, this became his method for ending the lives of patients.

Shipman was convicted of only 15 deaths but is suspected of up to 250 during his medical career. A home-visit doctor, many of his terminal patients died in their homes shortly after his visits. Some people have drawn parallels between Shipman and Jack Kevorkian, with the exception that Kevorkian was never known to pursue monetary gain.

Although not the only British doctor to be accused of killing his patients, as of 2022 he is the only one to ever be convicted.

Something superficial that probably helped Shipman avoid suspicion for so long was his physical appearance. Imagine the visual stereotype of the "kindly country doctor." That is how Shipman appeared. Killers are supposed to *look* evil, right? You can "see it in their eyes." If that was true, very few would be successful. When we look later at serial killers, despite the "crazed" photos media chooses in order to fit our perception of killers, in-person most serial killers look and act very normal. That is their power to attract victims.

Christine Malèvre a former nurse whose arrest spurred the kind of conversations in France that Jack Kevorkian's arrest did in the United States, was put on trial for killing seven terminal patients in 1997 and 1998. She is suspected in up to 30.

She claimed she had administered lethal doses of drugs at the request of terminally ill patients who wished to die. Many of the families later denied their loved ones would ever have made such requests.

We need to look at cultural and religious demographics in this case, especially when comparing Malèvre and Kevorkian. Nearly half of France identifies as Catholic, as did the majority of Malèvre's victims. Catholicism is very hostile toward the idea of euthanasia, so the public was more likely to side with families who said their loved ones would never make such a choice. Despite multiple attempts to bring Death with Dignity laws to France, as of 2022 all have failed.

Finally, let's really push the boundary on the definition of altruism:

Miyuki Ishikawa was a Japanese midwife and manager of a maternity hospital in the years during and after World War II. Her and her husband were accused in the deaths of at least 84 infants under their care. They were indicted for only 27 deaths, and ultimately convicted for the deaths of only five. The final sentence was four years for Miyuki and two years for her husband. Seem light? Let's get into the social and environmental issues surrounding this case.

The recovery of the Japanese economy after WWII is often called the "Japanese Economic Miracle," but those years near the end of the war and several years afterward were anything but a miracle, they were an economic disaster for many families at a time when the government had been encouraging parents to have large families. Abortion was illegal, and in 1930 the Ministry of Home Affairs had banned contraception. By 1937 had banned all information on contraception, arguing that a large increase in population would be necessary for the survival of the culture, especially as it entered the second world war.

This resulted in a spike of abandoned children at maternity hospitals, including the one managed by Miyuki Ishikawa. Not having the staff to care for so many babies, and viewing abandoned babies as fated for lives of pain and misery, Ishikawa engaged in what the court later called a "Crime of Omission;" removing care from many of the infants, allowing them to die.

This was not limited to children who had been abandoned at the facility, as a mid-wife she also killed babies shortly after birth if the mothers were financially unable to care for the child, and later was accused, along with her husband, of charging families for taking babies and killing them, under the rationale that the cost of termination was much less than the cost of raising a child.

At this point you can either see why I mentioned pushing the boundary of the definition of altruistic killing, or you are thinking there is no way this fits an altruistic mindset by any definition. Let me address why this can be defined as altruistic. Remember, altruism in a killer is defined by the perceptions and rationalizations of the killer, not by the objective reality of what they are doing. To Ishikawa she was saving children from lives of suffering, pain, torment, and probably early death given the social and economic conditions of the time. She was also saving parents the economic hardship of having to care for more children, a hardship that could drive them to economic collapse. From her perspective, ending the lives of the infants was doing the best thing for everyone involved.

Japanese society, and the government, did not entirely disagree. In 1949, a year after Ishikawa was given her four-year sentence, a revision to the Eugenics Protection Bill of 1948 made abortion legal in cases of extreme physical or economic distress to the mother. Can you see why social and government attitudes might have led to the light sentence?

Overlap and the Middle Ground:

We have looked at the three broad categories: Hero, Psychotic, and Altruistic, but you have probably noticed the individual cases often do not fit cleanly into single categories. There is often overlap, and over time someone might start with one motivation and evolve into another. Let's look at a few which blended categories.

Donald Harvey claimed to have killed up to 87 people between 1970 and 1987 while working as a hospital orderly. His career started at a hospital in Kentucky, where he claimed to have killed more than a dozen patients in just ten months, but most of his murders came as he bounced around facilities in Ohio, where he was eventually arrested.

Harvey claimed that in the beginning the killings were out of compassion, to end the suffering of terminally ill patients, but he admitted that as time went by he would also kill patients if they frustrated him or angered him in any way. This is obviously a crossover between the altruistic and psychotic categories. Nothing in his statements or victim profiling indicate a hero motivation, especially since he worked as an orderly and would have no viable role in saving anyone.

He was successful for so long because he did not leave a consistent trail. He used various poisons, sometimes shut off or disabled life-support equipment, and in some cases smothered victims with pillows. Because these patients were considered terminal and not expected to survive anyway, the deaths were not considered suspicious, and no autopsies were performed which could have revealed the presence of poisons. This might seem like a terrible medical oversight, but if someone is hospitalized with late-stage cancer, and is not expected to survive more than a couple months, and they die while in the hospital, it is usually safe to assume the cancer was the cause of death. There is little point in taking the time and expense of an autopsy to confirm what seems obvious.

In 1987, he was arrested when an autopsy was performed on one of his victims, John Powell, who had been on life support for several months following a motorcycle accident. In this case an autopsy was performed because the sudden death was inconsistent with the injuries and there were no signs of deterioration leading up to the death. The results found high concentrations of cyanide. It was not until an investigation started that the hospital discovered Harvey had been dismissed from his previous job for stealing body parts from the hospital. Why, you might ask, did they not check into him before hiring him in the first place? At the time the hospital did not check the backgrounds of orderlies with the same scrutiny applied to doctors and nurses. Harvey immediately became a prime suspect, and when questioned, confessed to the killing. A local journalist wondered if this was an isolated incident or if Harvey might have a history of this, and their inquiries led to tips from other medical professionals who had worked with him. As part of a plea agreement which allowed him to avoid the death penalty, Harvey eventually pled guilty to 24 killings in Ohio, and later an additional nine in Kentucky, but remained a suspect in many others which lacked sufficient evidence for conviction. He was incarcerated in Ohio in 1987.

Epilogue: In March 2017 he was found severely beaten in his cell and died two days later. His cellmate was convicted of the murder.

Efren Saldivar worked as a respiratory therapist from 1989 until 1998. Only charged with six murders which occurred in 1996 and 1997, he claims to have killed more than 50 during his career, starting just six months after his first job in 1989.

I put Saldivar in this category because he is sometimes thought of as an altruistic killer because his victims were all considered near death and were unconscious when he poisoned them. This is also why he managed to escape detection for so long, he was careful to make sure the rate of deaths at the facility were not substantially greater when he was on staff, and the deaths would not be considered suspicious, therefore it was unlikely there would be autopsies.

He does not fit hero because when possible he picked victims who had Do Not Resuscitate (DNR) orders, therefore there would be no opportunity to save them.

He best fits psychotic because his primary motivation seemed to be the thrill of being able to kill and get away with it. The fact that he might have been putting people out of their misery did not seem to be a motivating factor at all.

Let's finish with the worst case of healthcare murder in the last hundred years, and one in which those who participated rationalized it as altruistic.

Am Spiegelgrund Clinic in Vienna where between 1940 and 1945 at least 789 children and adolescents were killed for being sick and/or disabled, or if perfectly healthy in mind and body were considered for euthanizing based on being labeled "delinquent, inferior, or defective." How were these categories determined? Delinquent if the child was a runaway or involved in petty crime, inferior if born out of wedlock or came from poverty, and defective if the parents were alcoholics or criminals (Spiegelgrund Survivors Speak Out). And obviously, if a child was Jewish, any inferiority, real or imagined, would be reason for euthanizing.

How can people do this to children? It is unfortunately not hard to understand. This was part of the 20th Century "eugenics" movement which was not limited to the Nazis. There was a general "weed out the weak for the benefit of the majority" sentiment across much of the west, even in the United States. People with disabilities, either mental or physical, were considered less deserving of life, less likely to have a life of any value, and a burden on the rest of society. Even people who did not agree to the killing of such people quietly agreed with the judgement of their value as humans.

You can imagine if someone believes an individual has no future and will forever be a burden, it is merciful to end their life rather than force them to live a life of struggle as an outcast. What's more, if this is not only endorsed, but encouraged by the government, it is easy to rationalize it as correct and acceptable, not to mention, it washes one's hands of personal responsibility if it is being done by the command of an authority.

This was demonstrated by the experiments of Stanley Milgram at Yale University in the early 1960s (Milgram, 1974), in which a subject assigned as a "teacher" would read questions to an unseen "student" in another room. If the student answered wrong, the teacher delivered an electric shock as punishment. For each wrong answer, the voltage of the shock was increased. At one point the subject would ask to stop the experiment, but the "authority figure" in the room with the teacher would insist the experiment continue. At one point the student would stop responding at all, even as stronger and stronger shocks were delivered.

Of course, what the teacher did not know was that no shocks were really being delivered, the student was a lab assistant playing a scripted role. The goal of the experiment was to see if the teacher would give in to the pleas of the student and refuse to continue with the experiment, or give in to the authority figure and continue delivering shocks even when they feared they might be harming the student.

The results shocked many (pun intended). Around three-quarters of participants continued to the end of the experiment despite the student asking, then begging for them to stop, and continued even when the student stopped responding.

But there is a caveat. You can find videos from the experiment online, and if you watch extended versions you will notice the "teachers" did display distress, sometimes great distress, at what they were doing, and did continue under the insistence of the authority figure even though it was producing tremendous stress for them (this, by the way, is why the experiment is considered unethical. Even though they were debriefed afterward, and shown that they were not delivering real shocks, it did not counter the unethical distress they were put under during the experiment), at one point most participants ask the authority figure "Do you take responsibility?" to which the authority responds "yes."

And there we have a self-feeding circle. The person giving the order can at least partially shun responsibility because they are not the one carrying out the act, while the person carrying out the act feels less responsible because they are being ordered to and therefore are not personally responsible for their actions.

It is not hard to see how a "lack of responsibility" loop like this could get out of control and lead to horrific behavior that no one is attempting to stop.

This is at least part of what was going on at the Spiegelgrund facility; a mentality that it is better for these children and adolescents to not live, combined with the permission of authority to carry out the actions leading to their deaths.

To a lesser extent but more common, it is an extreme version of engaging in a behavior because of peer pressure, even though the behavior is distressing to you, as well as the influence of "mob mentality" to make an unacceptable behavior temporarily acceptable in the moment because others in the crowd are doing it and there is no personal responsibility for joining them.

On that happy note, it's time to dive into the mind of mass killers.

Chapter Seven

Mass shooters and School shooters

Mass shootings and their subset School shootings are easily the most terrifying of murder scenarios due to the number of victims, the seemingly randomness of the act, and the victims usually being strangers who happened to be in the wrong place at the wrong time.

They are also the easiest to understand and explain yet difficult to predict because so few of the people who display the profile ever hurt anyone. The motivating factors which make the difference are usually not apparent to those around the shooter and are quite often a simple matter of the shooter interpreting an external life event as catastrophic. At the end of this chapter I will cover social media posts preceding an attack as one way to potentially identify an escalating threat that might be unique to mass killers.

We have covered the base cognitions and attitudes in previous chapters: "If I'm going out, I'm taking someone with me." Have you ever had thoughts like that? If we knew an asteroid was going to strike the Earth next week and completely end humanity, do you think the murder rate would skyrocket over the next week? There would definitely be people out killing simply because there would be no consequence, and an escalation in suicides and murder/suicides by people who did not want to suffer through that final week; but do you think there would also be people deciding to take the opportunity to harm those who had wronged them? What keeps people from doing that now? Obviously, the law and the threat of prison, but also having to live with the consequences and experience the aftermath of what they did.

You can probably already see where we are going, but first we need to work through the definitions of different categories of shootings and the labels applied to the shooters because they can cast a very broad umbrella which often includes incidents you would not think to put in the category of a Mass Shooting or School Shooting.

A **Mass Shooting** involves three or more victims at one time and in one place. We would call it Mass Murder if there are multiple victims, or simply Mass Shooting if there are multiple injuries but no deaths.

A **Spree Killer** also requires three or more victims, but the period can be up to 30 days and involve multiple locations. Often the killings are connected to another crime, such as robbery. When you hear something reported as a "crime spree" which also involves deaths, it would qualify as a spree killing. For example: Nineteen-year-old Charles Starkweather and his 14-year-old girlfriend Caril Fugate went on a month-long killing spree across Nebraska and Wyoming in 1958 after killing Fugate's parents and sister. They were the inspiration for the movie "Natural Born Killers" in 1994. Starkweather had been teased mercilessly as a kid due to a speech impediment, and a birth defect which gave him "bow-legs." He later became obsessed with working out, to the point he could physically start bullying the people who had once bullied him. According to friends and family he became prone to violent outbursts, dropped out of school, and committed his first murder less than two months before the killing spree began. It was never certain whether Caril was a willing participant or a hostage. She was sentenced to life in prison for her participation but was paroled in 1976, and in 2020 attempted, and failed, to have the court clear her of the earlier charges. Charles fits our profile of both rage and desire for revenge. It is unknown whether the spree was suicidal in motivation. He was sentenced to death and was executed in June 1959.

An **Active Shooter** is very simply an individual actively engaged in killing or attempting to kill people in a populated area. Keep in mind, this definition is based on how the shooter is perceived in the moment, not their actual intent. Meaning, someone might be shooting in self-defense, but to those around them they appear to be targeting innocent people. A good example of this grey area is Kenosha, Wisconsin in August 2020 when violence erupted over the police shooting of Jacob Blake and several buildings were burned during the unrest. On the second night of protests armed groups arrived to protect businesses and property. One of these was 17-year-old Kyle Rittenhouse, who had driven to Kenosha with his mother from their home in Illinois. During the evening Kyle was chased by a protestor and shot the man, killing him instantly. Rittenhouse then ran toward a police line more than a block away. A small group of protesters down the street, having heard the initial shots being fired, saw an armed man being chased up the street by a crowd shouting that he had shot someone. When they tried to stop Rittenhouse, he shot one to death and injured another before continuing past the police line to a business his mother and some others had been guarding. After firing the first shot, Rittenhouse was by any definition an active shooter. No one away from the shooting, including the police stationed along their line, knew the reason Rittenhouse had fired those first shots and then fled. The shots, as recorded by live streamers at the time, could be heard more than a block away. After-the-fact, Rittenhouse and his legal team claimed self-defense as the motivation, but no one present at the second shooting location knew the circumstances; they simply knew this person had shot someone and was running toward them. A person stops being an active shooter when they either leave the area or are detained by police.

School Shooting is a shooting on school property. The definition is broader than what we think when we hear about a school shooting. When someone says "School Shooting" we think of an armed person going into a school during school hours with the intent of killing students. In this scenario a school shooter is also an active shooter and will be labeled as such by responding law enforcement. But the general definition of school shooting is much broader. It is simply the illegal discharge of a firearm on school property. It does not require that people be present, or any person be a target. Shots being fired into the air in a school parking lot after a high school sports event is technically a school shooting. A lone person shooting out windows of an empty school in the middle of the night is a school shooting. This is how school shooting numbers can be so high while the number of active shooter events resulting in injury or death are so small by comparison. It is not that people intentionally misuse the statistics to exaggerate the threat, they are simply applying their interpretation of school shooting to statistics that include much more.

Obviously, school shooting is a subset of mass shooting, but are there differences between them? Some. But we will start with how they are similar, because the cognitions and motivations overlap. An adult mass shooter is in many ways someone who, if the circumstances had been right, could have been a school shooter when they were younger. For example: Payton Gendron, the 18-year-old who carried out the supermarket shooting in Buffalo New York in May 2022 admitted that he had earlier planned a school shooting.

In chapter three I covered revenge fantasies. Such fantasies are very common and are considered one of the ways we emotionally heal from traumatic events. Most people will never act on them, and over time they will begin to diminish. If they do not diminish over time, or the person becomes more obsessed with them, that's a warning sign, and the first part of our mass/shooter school/shooter formula.

The second ingredient? Suicidal ideation. And here is where we come back to the statement at the beginning of the chapter. "I'm going out and I'm taking someone with me." If your life is going to end, your actions carry no personal consequence. It makes sense you might think about taking out a person or persons you felt did you wrong or hurt you in some way.

As I mentioned earlier, this is the same cognition that motivates murder/suicide. Mass shooting and school shooting have the same murder/suicide mentality, the difference is whether the target is a single person or small number of people versus a larger group or entire demographic.

If suicidal ideation is one of the key components, why are there so many mass shooters and school shooters who do not end their lives? Thinking about, or even planning suicide is still several cognitive and emotional steps away from being able to carry out the act, which is why so many people who want to end their lives will find a passive way to do it, such as "suicide by cop" where they force police to shoot them. And as we will see in a moment, sometimes the reality of the moment does not fit the fantasy the person has built around it and their plans will change. The ability to end your own life can be a very short moment, and anything that interrupts the moment can change the willingness or ability to follow through with self-harm.

There is also a cognitive parallel to suicide: Giving up on life. Rather than suicide, this could mean surrendering personal freedom and giving up on any long-term goals. Throwing in the towel and letting whatever happens to you happen. There are people who want to live to see the result of their actions and truly do not care what happens to them afterward.

Thomas M. "T.J." Lane III was a 17-year-old student at Lake Academy in Willoughby Ohio. Lake Academy was an alternative school for students with academic or behavioral issues. Before attending Lake Academy, Lane had attended Chardon High School in nearby Chardon Ohio. Lane was among several students who would catch a bus from Chardon to Lake Academy each day. On February 27, 2012 Lane showed up at Chardon armed. He went into the cafeteria and shot six students, three of whom later died. Police later found him waiting by his car in the school parking lot, making no effort to escape. He claimed he picked victims at random, but students familiar with him said he had multiple past conflicts with the first victim and was likely targeting him. Lane was given three life sentences and at his sentencing hearing took off his shirt to reveal a tee-shirt with "Killer" written across it, then laughed at the victims' families while giving them the middle finger (Cleveland19.com, 2016). In 2014 he briefly escaped and was then moved to a maximum-security facility, where he continues to be defiant toward any sort of authority or rules.

Lane is a classic case of someone who feels wronged or controlled by "the system" and therefore decides to violate the norms and rules of the system whenever possible and considers arrest and jail to be a victory. He gave up any expectation of a normal life, and before taking that final step chose to target someone who he felt had wronged him.

Another example is a little more complex. James Holmes, who on July 20, 2012 killed 12 people and wounded 70 others at a theater in Aurora Colorado. He is outside the norm of mass shooters in a couple ways: He did not target a specific demographic, he was simply looking for a crowd, and the impulse and fantasy of carrying out a mass killing had been with him for many years. For at least a year before the shootings he cycled between suicidal and homicidal drives. His plans at different points included the possibility of escape and at others a shoot-out with police. He had thought about targeting the airport but was afraid people would assume he was a terrorist, which indicates he was at least partially motivated by how the act would be perceived afterward. He decided on a theater because he said he liked theaters. He chose the Dark Knight film because he knew the theater would be crowded, and he chose the midnight showing because he assumed there would be fewer children in the theater, and he did not want to shoot children. He chose the specific theater due to the police response time, giving him time to shoot as many people as possible and still have opportunity to escape. On the night of the shooting he wore an urban assault vest. He exited the theater through a back entrance, propped the door open, and retrieved the weapons from his car. He returned and released gas or smoke into the theater before he started shooting.

And here is what I mean when I mentioned earlier that the reality might not match the fantasy. Long before police arrived, and still with ammunition and victims available, he stopped, went out the back exit and waited by his car for police to arrive. Not only did he surrender without incident, he warned police he had rigged his apartment with explosives. Mental health experts who studied him later diagnosed him with a range of dysfunctions: schizophrenia, schizoid personality disorder, schizoaffective disorder, and psychosis at the time of the shooting. But here is the problem with all of those. Holmes had shown tendencies throughout his life which could reflect schizoaffective disorder and perhaps schizoid personality disorder, but we must consider the cognitive effect of carrying out the murders. When he got a good look at the reality of what he was doing, he stopped. He gave up. And according to those who did the initial interrogation he was experiencing an active psychotic episode. It is unlikely he could have planned out the shooting over such an extended period and with such detail if he was overwhelmed by a psychosis. It is more likely the psychotic break was the result of the shootings. Sitting out by his car waiting for police was not in any of his original planning. If he did not choose to escape, he was going to kill himself or die in a shoot-out with police. After being arrested he did attempt suicide several times and had to be put on suicide watch.

If he had these thoughts and impulses for years prior to the event, what finally pushed him toward doing it? He claims it was a break-up the previous winter. He started dating a fellow student in October 2011. It ended in December, then briefly resumed in January before ending again in February. According to the student Holmes wanted a serious relationship, but she wanted something more casual; they had an ongoing "friends with benefits" relationship into the spring (News Corp, 2015). In either March or April, he started buying rounds of ammunition, and in May and June, he began purchasing the weapons. Is such a short relationship likely to send him to such an extreme? It is, depending on how emotionally invested he became and how he handled the break-up. By the girlfriend's account Holmes showed signs of extreme jealousy very early on, possibly leading to the first break-up. He would become agitated when other men talked to her. This is a serious red flag at any point in a relationship, but especially if it happens early. To add to the conflict of his desire for a serious relationship versus her desire for something more casual, it was Holmes' first sexual experience. The emotional imprint of that is tremendous.

Why did Holmes not target her specifically rather than a theater of strangers? Very likely he wanted her to witness the aftermath and feel partially responsible for the killings as a way of punishing her for rejecting him.

A different example that displays the primary similarity between mass shooters and school shooters is Connor Betts. In August of 2019, when Betts was 24 years old, he killed nine people and wounded 17 others in a shooting outside a bar in Dayton, Ohio. He had obsessed about mass shootings since his early teens and had been suspended in high school for putting together a "kill list" of students. It is very likely the only reason he was not a school shooter was the absence of a precipitating event to push him over the edge. What was the precipitating event on the night of August 4, 2019 that finally pushed him to that extreme? Two things, the effects of alcohol and drugs earlier in the evening, and an event that happened in El Paso, Texas 13 hours earlier when Patrick Wood Crusius walked into a Wal-Mart Supercenter and opened fire, killing 22 people and injuring another 23 before surrendering to police. Crusius himself was inspired by the Christchurch shootings in New Zealand earlier that year in which 51 people were killed. Both of those mass shootings fall into the subset of "hate crime" because they target a demographic based on a specific hatred of the group rather than a personal vendetta. Crusius posted an anti-Latino manifesto before the shooting and, like James Holmes, was found in a psychotic state when he surrendered to police after the shooting. In the case of Connor Betts, there is no indication he was targeting any specific group but it is possible a person or persons at the bar were specific targets and we will never know because they were killed, and Connor himself was shot dead by police within 30 seconds of the start of the shooting.

Like many mass and school shooters, Connor Betts had a history of being bullied in school. This is likely where he developed an interest in mass shootings fueled by his own ongoing revenge fantasies.

We need to step back for a moment because I just made a loaded insinuation by associating bullying with becoming a mass or school shooter. It is obviously more complex than that one correlation. Many people get bullied. According to Stopbullying.gov around 19% nationwide in the United States each year. Most do not turn into criminals, most do not develop suicidal ideation, but the psychological effects of bullying contribute to multiple factors which influence those, such as anxiety, depression and feelings of despair and isolation. School support, peer support, and family support also play a factor in the degree to which bullying will emotionally impact an individual, so you can imagine how hard it would be to predict a specific outcome such as suicide or homicide when so many factors must converge.

Our two broad factors of obsessive, ongoing revenge fantasies and suicidal ideation are comprised of many components, and thankfully, of the millions of people who experience the environmental influences which can lead to these tragic results, only a small percentage experience the unfortunate joining of all these factors.

So, when I say mass and school shooters have histories of being bullied, it is true. But there were a variety of other factors at work as well. Too many to put together a predictive profile. For example. I cannot predict the long-term outcome of a single student being bullied, but I can guess the root experiences of a mass shooter.

There is another stereotype we need to address. When you hear about bullying you probably think of school age children, specifically Middle School and High School where bullying seems to be the worse. But bullying occurs in adulthood too. We are familiar with it even if only through media, we see it in movies and on TV all the time, but we rarely think about it when we think of "bullying." Mostly because it is more often labeled as "harassment."

Adults will bully for the same reasons children bully: Because someone looks different, sounds different, or acts different. And bullies across the board share the common trait of insecurity and a need to feel in control. Bullying results from a need to feel dominant, but the presence of insecurity means the desire for dominance will focus on those perceived as easy targets. Bullies do not focus on those who appear strong, they focus on those who are perceived as passive or weak.

Adult bullying is not a new area of study. Back in 1976 Carroll Brodsky in *The Harassed Worker* provided a definition of adult harassment which sounds very much like schoolyard bullying: "repeated and persistent attempts by one person to torment, wear down, frustrate, or get a reaction from another. It is treatment which persistently provokes, pressures, frightens, intimidates or otherwise discomforts another person" (p.2). Furthermore, he recognized two subcategories which often overlap: Subjective Harassment meaning the target is aware of the harassment, and Objective Harassment, meaning there is external evidence of the harassment.

The key is whether the target recognizes the harassment and to what degree it impacts them. Obviously different people will have different thresholds and different ways of either coping with, or completely dismissing harassment.

Harassers will hide behind the excuse of "joking" even though their intent is to insult or harm. This puts additional pressure on the target by making them appear "thin-skinned, overly sensitive" or someone who simply "can't take a joke." This often keeps the target from saying anything about how the behavior is hurting them, and rather than looking for external solutions they do a slow internal burn. Obviously, it is impossible to see from the outside how harassment is emotionally landing on someone unless they say something about it.

And guess what? This can be the root of creating revenge fantasies which can escalate as the harassment continues. Adult bullying runs the gambit of name-calling, intimidation, humiliation, devaluation, undue pressure, or impossible deadlines meant to produce failure and then blaming the failure on the target.

It was never absolutely determined, but workplace harassment by peers and supervisors was thought to be a primary factor in the case of Patrick Sherrill. Have you ever heard the expression "going postal" in reference to workplace shootings or in general losing control and becoming violent? This started with Sherrill, who in August 1986 killed fourteen co-workers, including a supervisor, and injured six others at the post office in Edmond Oklahoma where he worked. It is still the deadliest workplace shooting in U.S. history, and might have spawned a series of copycat shootings. From 1991 to 2006 there were seven other workplace shootings involving postal workers, reinforcing a stereotype, played for laughs with the character "Newman" on several episodes of the TV series "Seinfeld" that the majority of postal workers were stressed, overworked, and just one step away from "going postal."

Is there a better way to identify mass shooting threats before they act? In the age of social media there is a difference in mass shooters and school shooters today compared to the decades prior to the Columbine shootings: They talk about their plans on social media. Sometimes this starts as passing remarks that can easily be dismissed as isolated throwaway comments you would expect from anyone, but over time the comments will become more frequent and more detailed.

When we treat a client for depression, one of the warning signs of escalating suicidal ideation is the formulation of a plan. Thinking about how they would do it even if they are not currently at a point to carry it out. Mass shooters seem to be similar. Does this mean at some level they want to be caught? No. It means they are playing out a fantasy, cognitively rehearsing and reinforcing the act until they push themselves to the point of carrying it out.

Elliot Rodger was a Christmas tree of warning signs in this way. As was Nikolas Cruz, the Parkland shooter in 2018, and the Buffalo supermarket and Uvalde school shooters in May 2022. In recent years measures have been put in place to respond to these threats before they escalate to violence, but authorities do not always follow through.

Let's turn our focus to school shooting specifically because it has its own history and is the greater focus of public attention and concern.

Contrary to what some people believe, school shootings are not a modern phenomenon. What has mostly changed since the 1990s are the types of weapons used, the number of victims, and the quantity and length of media attention. But there were two other key changes we will get to shortly.

Prior to Columbine, most school shootings had specific targets, such as a specific, student, faculty, or administrator, and most were carried out with the common weapons of the time, a handgun or hunting rifle. Rarely did they target a larger student demographic. They would receive local media attention but rarely, if ever, did they receive national attention. Let's dive a little deeper into that last point.

In 1966 there was no internet, no social media, no 24/7 cable news channels. Your source for televised national news was a half-hour program in the evening. Your local and regional papers would cover some national headlines, but they mostly emphasized more local stories, filling in with national stories if they had extra space to fill. National radio news broadcasts were five to ten minutes, so networks had to be selective about what they covered. There was no way to cover every "big" story with such little time.

On August 1, 1966, Charles Whitman carried seven weapons up to the observation deck on the 27th floor of "The Tower" at the University of Texas in Austin. From this position he began targeting people on the street below. Over the span of 90 minutes he killed 14 people and injured 31 before finally being shot by police and a private citizen. Up to that time it was the deadliest mass shooting in U.S. history. The next day it dominated most local, regional, and national news programs and newspapers. But it quickly disappeared from media over the following days in favor of other stories. There was not enough available time to give it ongoing coverage. If you had not paid attention to the news the day after it happened, you might never have heard about it.

On the morning of January 29, 1979 16-year-old Brenda

Spencer, who lived across the street from the Grover Cleveland Elementary School in San Diego, shot at children waiting for the school principal to open the front gates to let them into the school. Eight children and a police officer were injured; the principal and a custodian were killed. This was a one-minute story in national media, not covered at all in many local papers outside of Southern California. If you lived on the east coast at the time you might have never heard of the case.

Ten years later, on January 17, 1989, at a school with coincidentally the same name but in Stockton California, Patrick Purdy opened fire on a school playground killing five children and wounding 32. This shooting would get more media coverage than the others because of the number of dead and wounded, and this shooting would be referenced frequently as support for the ten-year assault weapons ban which was passed five years later in 1994.

There was similar time-limited coverage of the San Ysidro massacre in 1984 where James Huberty opened fire in a McDonalds, killing 21 and wounding 19, and the Luby's restaurant shooting in Killeen Texas in 1991 where George Hennard drove his pickup through the front window of Luby's and then opened fire on employees and customers, killing 23 and wounding 27. Both received national coverage, but like other shootings, the networks shortly moved on to other stories. Back in 1949 there was even less national coverage of the "Walk of Death" when Howard Unruh, who by today's standards was suffering from severe untreated PTSD resulting from World War Two, went casually strolling through his Camden New Jersey neighborhood shooting everyone he saw, killing thirteen people (including three children) and injuring three. If in the 1950s you had asked people about the Camden shooting most people would probably say they never heard of it.

These examples represent the *major* shooting events. Lesser events received little or no national coverage at all, and usually only regional coverage in the areas where the shootings occurred. You think there were no school shootings back in the nostalgic 70s and 80s? In the 1970s there were 40 school shootings involving death or injury, accounting for a total of 39 dead and 79 injured. In the 1980s it climbed to 60 shootings, accounting for 66 dead and 188 injured, not counting 71 killed and 27 injured in five non-school mass shooting incidents. If you were a teen or adult in those years Google the list and see how many you remember.

National media back then did not have the infrastructure to give continuing coverage or create ongoing conversations around these attacks like mass media and social media have today.

What changed everything, both in media coverage and method of attack, was Columbine on April 20, 1999 when Eric Harris and Dylan Klebold roamed the halls of Columbine High School in Colorado for 50 minutes, killing a teacher and 12 students, and injuring 21 others before taking their own lives.

Columbine by itself was not the catalyst that brought a flood of media attention. It was the fifth (and deadliest) school shooting in the previous 18 months and recognized as a sign the problem was rapidly escalating. Most people have heard of Columbine, but unless you lived in an area where regional media covered these other stories you have probably not heard of them.

On October 1, 1997, 16-year-old Luke Woodham, a junior at Pearl Harbor High School in Pearl Mississippi, and a member of a group at the school called "The Kroth" killed his mother, then went to school and opened fire, killing two students and injuring seven others. He was captured in the parking lot trying to escape. Six other members of the Kroth at the school were arrested for conspiracy to commit murder. The group, like online Incel groups today, would meet and discuss violent attacks. The group had groomed Woodham to initiate the attack, possibly leading him to believe others would join him.

Two months later, on December 1, 1997, 14-year-old Michael Carneal, a freshman at Heath High School in West Paducah Kentucky, snuck several weapons into the school wrapped in a blanket, claiming they were materials for an art project, then opened fire on a youth group, killing three and injuring five. He then surrendered his weapons to the principal, saying "Kill me, please. I can't believe I did that." When a copy of Stephen King's novel "Rage" was found in his locker (initially published under the name Richard Bachman and included in early printings of "The Bachman Books"), King requested the book be pulled from publication, and later had it removed from "The Bachman Books."

Less than three months later, on March 24, 1998, two middle school students: 13-year-old Mitchell Johnson and 11-year-old Andrew Golden, planned to steal Johnson's mother's van, load it with weapons and survival supplies from their homes, carry out a shooting at their school and then use the van to run away from home. They drove to the middle school and hid the weapons in woods near the school, then went inside the school, pulled the fire alarm, and ran back to their weapons. Hiding in the woods they started firing at students after they had evacuated the school. They killed four students and a teacher and injured 10 others. They were captured later trying to flee in the van. Both came from divorced households and had displayed a pattern of increased aggression toward others which had not been addressed by either the school or their parents. Mass shootings involving multiple shooters are very rare, and given this shooting occurred just 13 months before Columbine it is likely it influenced Klebold and Harris. And like the Columbine shooters, the shooting probably would not have happened if the two had been separated at any time prior to their plans escalating to murder.

The last shooting leading up to Columbine was just two months later. On May 21, 1998, Kip Kinkel, a 15-year-old student at Thurston High School in Springfield Oregon, who had been suspended the previous day for bringing a loaded, stolen gun to school, killed his parents, then drove to the high school where he opened fire, killing two and injuring 25 before being tackled by a student while pausing to reload.

As was the case with earlier shootings, these four received mostly regional media coverage, and some national coverage, but Columbine was the first mass shooting of the cable-news and internet era to get obsessive coverage and online chatter for days and weeks afterward. This meant, forever after, mass shootings and school shootings would get extensive national coverage unlike any before, and unfortunately serve as a blueprint for later shooters. Prior to Columbine, shooters were focused primarily on their targets, not on the expectation of media coverage. After Columbine there was an increase in shooters who were expecting the media coverage.

Standard police response also changed. Active shooter protocol at the time was to contain active shooters, but after Columbine it became more common to adopt an Immediate Action Rapid Deployment tactic in which police would more aggressively enter a facility in pursuit of the shooters. This was adopted after public outcry over the timeline of the Columbine shooting when the public learned that the shooters were dead an hour before the first SWAT team entered the building. It was obvious some victims were killed and injured while police were positioned outside the school, and some victims died due to the delay in allowing paramedics into the facility. Unfortunately, even when trained on this tactic, not all police departments follow it when faced with an active shooter event.

What about the Columbine shooters? Was there an obvious progression toward their final acts? Yes, and like Westside Middle School, it is unique because it involves two friends progressing together both fueling and reinforcing their anger. This is an important point I will repeat several times because it is likely that if they had been separated at any point, neither alone would have carried out the attack.

Eric Harris came from a very traditional and conservative active military family, meaning his mother was a homemaker and the family moved around a lot as the father was stationed at different locations. The most common social risk that comes out of this environment is an inability to develop and maintain long-term friendships, obviously because of frequent relocation. This frequent loss of friends created resentment in Harris, who blamed his father for these losses. He was in middle school when his father retired, and the family settled permanently in Littleton Colorado.

Dylan Klebold came from what is described as a pacifist household and devoutly Lutheran, but he did seem to be more of a dependent personality and occasional depressive which would have made him an easy target to be influenced by a more dominant peer.

The two met in middle school and formed a tight friendship. It was during this time that Harris began to voice anger toward society, and some of this he vented in online posts. His rants became more specifically violent, including fantasizing about killing people he interacted with online. This led to him being reported, and an investigation being planned but never carried out. Harris and Klebold began to experiment with petty crimes culminating in an arrest for breaking into a van and stealing various items. They were sentenced to a "juvenile diversion" program including anger management classes.

Given their later actions, it is easy to assume these programs were useless, but again, the failure was in their ongoing self-perpetuating spiral. If either of their parents had separated the pair after the arrest, the attacks would have been less likely. On the surface it seems like Harris was the driving force, and destined to have run-ins with the law, and Klebold would have likely wandered into other friendships or spent the rest of his high school years mostly isolated socially; but it is hard to extract their mutual reinforcement from the equation. Klebold was the more passive of the two, but this might have been the kind of silent endorsement that fueled Harris. In other words, which is more responsible for the music, the instrument or the musician? You cannot remove either and still have music.

Let's back up for a moment because I just breezed past a point that probably drew your attention. What was it about middle school and finally forming a stable friendship that could have fueled hostility in Eric Harris? I mentioned that Harris was hurt by frequently losing friends and blamed his father for it. In his writings he reported being decimated every time he heard the words "we're moving" (Santiago, 2019). But this is not uncommon, and although there are social issues and frequent teen rebellion among "military brats" they do not display a significantly higher rate of crime or antisocial behavior than the general population (so long as the parent who served does not display signs of PTSD, which can escalate dysfunctional behavior in the home and result in lashing out externally). Nothing in the history of Harris' father indicates he suffered from PTSD or was abusive in the home. The problem is his parents might have existed on the opposite extreme of the spectrum: Ignoring the escalating signs of trouble or refusing to believe them. As Eric Harris started to get in more trouble, his father maintained a journal simply titled "Eric" in which he documented his sons' behavior and the accusations against him (Santiago, 2019) but at the same time dismissed these accusations and accused others of being the problem by targeting or attempting to control his son. The most revealing evidence that such denial was a conscious attempt to hide the truth from himself was his 9-1-1 call on the day of the Columbine attack, before the shooters had been identified, when he told police he was afraid his son was one of the shooters. In fact, police came to the home and began collecting evidence (including explosives and other materials for making bombs) even before the bodies of Harris and Klebold had been discovered.

Here is a pattern we have seen before, and one we will see frequently in the next chapter: The behavior was allowed to escalate uninterrupted by people in the immediate environment who had the opportunity to address it. Because the family had moved so frequently (by the age of twelve Harris had attended five different schools) Harris never had an opportunity to find a peer who could actively or passively give his rage fertile ground to grow. In Klebold he found that peer.

Columbine was also unique in having multiple shooters, and in the magnitude of actual and intended destruction. They had brought propane tanks to use as bombs, and Molotov cocktails, intending to cause a major fire throughout the school. Their bombs did not go off, and the cocktails were extinguished by the sprinkler system.

The aftermath of Columbine put a new media and public paradigm in place for the reporting and reaction of not just school shootings, but mass shootings in general, regardless of the number of casualties. Shootings which previously received little or no national attention were starting to get more attention. In the eight years following Columbine there were 47 different school shooting incidents, with a cumulative total of 56 killed and 88 injured. These were mostly shootings in which the shooter sought out a few specific targets at the schools, usually a student or faculty, and cases in which the shootings occurred on school property but not within the school. It would be almost exactly eight years to the day before the horror of Columbine was overshadowed.

On April 16, 2007 Seung-Hui Cho, a student at Virginia Tech in Blacksburg Virginia, killed 32 students and faculty and injured 17 others in two separate attacks over the span of almost three hours. He started in the morning with what seemed a specific target, a student in her dorm room, then killed a resident assistant who responded to the sound of the shot (Follow-up investigations found no known connection between him and the victim).

He then went back to his dorm, changed his clothes, wiped out his emails and deleted his university account, then disposed of his phone and hard drive (they were never found). He stopped at the post office and mailed a manifesto and series of recorded videos to a network news outlet, then returned to the campus and carried out the second shooting in Norris Hall, a classroom building which housed Engineering, Science, and Mechanics. He used chains and locks to close the main entrances to the building, then went up to the second floor and began targeting classrooms. His victims were primarily in four classrooms, and several times he returned to the classrooms to shoot injured survivors. When police finally entered the building and were making their way to the second floor, Cho shot himself before they could engage him.

His pattern upon entering each room was identical, he shot the instructor first, then students. In two cases students attempted to barricade the doors but Cho either physically forced, or shot his way in.

Police had not locked down or issued any alerts to the campus after the first shooting because they assumed it was an isolated event likely related to a specific domestic dispute.

Initial reports after the shooting, and even Cho's anger-laden videos, suggested a history of bullying. But later investigations could find no evidence of the bullying Cho was referencing.

Who was Seung-Hui Cho? I should note first, the measures that are in place in the United States today would identify and stop a person with a similar risk profile from reaching this point (if the measures are followed).

Cho was born in 1984 in South Korea, his family moved to the United States when he was eight years old. There were concerns about Cho's developmental health from a very young age, with his family in South Korea noting that as a young child he did not make eye contact, did not show affection nor did he reciprocate displays of emotion. As an elementary school student in the U.S. he was very good academically but it was noted that he frequently did not respond verbally to teachers or other students, and when he did attempt to interact he displayed problems with interaction and social communication, such as not knowing how to properly initiate communication with others, appearing awkward, and frequently not completing sentences.

By eighth grade Cho was diagnosed with selective mutism, a social anxiety disorder in which a person verbally freezes in certain contexts or around unfamiliar people. He had unusual speech mannerisms (not specified in the reports released to the public) which led to being teased in middle school, continuing into high school.

Cho was in ninth grade in 1999 when the Columbine attack occurred. In a school assignment he wrote about having a desire to "repeat Columbine" and reportedly idolized the Columbine shooters. As a result, he was referred to a psychiatrist.

Cho's parents were initially very active in getting him help. Upon receiving the first diagnosis of selective mutism they sought both medication and therapy for treatment. It is unknown, however, how much help they provided in the home environment, or the specific conditions in the home. His parents owned and operated a dry-cleaning business, which consumed much of their time.

In high school he was placed in special education where he was excused from oral presentations or being required to participate in class conversations. He received speech therapy and mental health care until the end of his junior year.

Federal law prevented any of Cho's mental health history from being passed on to Virginia Tech without his permission, so when he enrolled, they had no idea he might have special needs.

Let's pause and roll back to a couple questions you probably have. Does his quick obsession with the Columbine shooters tell us anything about his mindset at the time, and why was autism-spectrum not considered as a diagnosis considering that he seems to be a hit on the main diagnostic criteria, and could misdiagnosis have caused more harm than good?

Cho no doubt had a consistently rough time throughout school, one of his first neighbors after starting elementary school reported that he would frequently have loud tantrums upon coming home from school, announcing he never wanted to go back.

And what is one of our first components of a mass shooter? Ongoing and escalating revenge fantasies. Klebold and Harris no doubt represented a fantasy of what Cho wanted to do to the classmates who teased him. This by itself is not enough to create a mass shooter, because as we noted earlier, many kids are teased or bullied in school without becoming violent. But it is an early indication of how frustrated he was, and how much anger was already brewing.

As for an autism-spectrum diagnosis, we must consider the time period. Autism as a term was first used in 1911 by the German psychiatrist Eugen Bleuler who was attempting to label specific symptoms of severe schizophrenia (Evans, 2013). Kanner (1943) first described what would today be the severe end of the autism spectrum in children, and a year later Asperger (1944) would describe what is today the high functioning end of the spectrum (the disorder to carry his name was not coined until several decades later). As late as the 1970s autism was not a widely accepted diagnosis and was still attached to the broader umbrella of schizophrenia. Even when "Autism" appeared in the third edition of the Diagnostic and Statistical Manual of Mental Disorders (DSM) in 1980 it was still exclusively the most severe end of the spectrum. During the 1980s evidence was growing that autism was a spectrum disorder, but it was not until the fourth edition of the DSM in 1994 that the spectrum was formally recognized. Even then, it took years before it was being widely recognized and applied.

The clinicians who originally diagnosed Cho with selective mutism might have been correct or might not. At that time autism was still frequently overlooked in favor of the older, more familiar diagnostic labels. If Cho was a better fit for the autism spectrum it could most certainly have meant the counseling and medication he was receiving for a diagnosis of selective mutism might not have been helpful, and indeed, might have magnified his frustration.

For example, if someone suffered from extreme anxiety, and the anxiety created an environment which led to depression, the primary focus of treatment should be the anxiety (get rid of the anxiety so the environment can improve, and the depression should recede). But if a clinician ignores the anxiety and focuses instead on the depression, not only will it not solve the problem, but it could allow the problem to escalate unchallenged.

At Virginia Tech several of Cho's instructors described him as arrogant, obnoxious, intimidating, and menacing. They found his writing very disturbing. His department head at one point contacted police about Cho's writing, but because it contained no specific threats against students or faculty, they could do nothing about it. Roommates found him awkward, strange, and sometimes frightening, and by their own admission attempted to avoid him. Cho was reported to campus police for stalking several female students, and on one occasion went into a female student's dorm room to "look in her eyes." Each time, campus police contacted Cho and ordered him to stay away from the reporting students. Each time he complied. After multiple incidents, including a statement by Cho that "I might as well kill myself," his parents were contacted and he was taken by police to a psychiatric hospital where a physician determined he was in need of hospitalization and was a likely threat to himself or others. A Judge ordered Cho to outpatient treatment, but no one ever followed through on the order. Throughout 2006 Cho's mother turned her attention to Churches to help Cho, deciding whatever was wrong with him could only be helped with "spiritual power." Little else was done to either help or detain him.

It is not hard to see that the red flags were there for several years, and it is surprising he was able to make it to his senior year at Virginia Tech without being expelled. The videos he recorded prior to the shootings and sent to media contain angry venting at no one in particular, shouting "you made me do this!" And as some have noted in the almost stream-of-consciousness and repetitive patterns of his rants he seemed a blend of schizophrenia and autism-spectrum disorder.

Over the following decade the number of shootings began to increase, with the ten worst attacks accounting for 237 deaths and 615 injuries. The Virginia Tech shooting was at the time the deadliest mass shooting in U.S. history, eventually surpassed by the Pulse nightclub shooting in 2016 which killed 49 and injured 58, then surpassed a year later by the Las Vegas shooting in Paradise, Nevada in 2017 which killed 60 and injured 411.

Virginia Tech also kick-started the resurgence of the gun-control debate, coming three years after the assault weapons ban had been lifted, and a year before a Presidential election. Gun control became a key politicized point for both sides during the election.

I introduced Virginia Tech by noting that precautions in place today would make it unlikely for a person with Cho's history and behavior to get as far as he did. But there is a sad caveat to that: The precautions need to be followed. Case in point: Stoneman Douglas High School in Parkland, Florida.

On the afternoon of February 14, 2018, Nikolas Cruz, who had been expelled the previous year, was seen arriving on campus with a backpack and rifle case. He entered a three-story classroom building (building 12) and begin indiscriminately shooting at teachers and students. Over the span of just six minutes he moved through the three floors of the building, killing 17 and wounding another 17 before dropping his weapons and blending in with other evacuating students. More than an hour later he was spotted in a nearby neighborhood and arrested. Upon initial interrogation he seemed somewhat disoriented and frequently repeated "Just kill me" (Johnson, 2018).

Before I go into his history of mental health and behavioral problems (and it is extensive) there is an obvious tipping point in the case of Cruz: His mother died three months before the shooting and the family who initially took him in very quickly kicked him out.

Cruz was born in 1998 and adopted at birth. His biological father is unknown, and his mother had a recurring drug problem, including a cocaine arrest while she was pregnant, likely having an impact on his biological development. Her next child, by a different father, was adopted at birth by the same family who adopted Cruz. The younger brother did not display any developmental issues.

Cruz was first diagnosed with "developmental delays" when he was three years old. When he was five, he witnessed his father die of a heart attack in the family home. He received a laundry list of diagnoses from childhood into the teen years, including autism spectrum disorder, depression, attention deficit hyperactivity disorder, emotional behavioral disability, obsessive-compulsive disorder and anger issues

(Wallman, et al., 2018). From an early age he was described as socially awkward, which often led to being teased, and had difficulty making friends. During his preteen and teen years he was known to be physically aggressive with the family when frustrated, the Sheriff's department later said they responded to 23 calls to the home over the span of 10 years due to violent outbursts. He was juggled among multiple schools due to behavioral problems, inappropriate language, and aggressive outbursts. Held back twice due to poor performance, he resented being in special education programs, he wanted to be mainstreamed into his local high school: Marjory Stoneman Douglas. Through middle school into early high school he began to demonstrate and verbalize obsessions with violence and guns, and hatred toward a variety of minority groups. At the start of his sophomore year of high school, he was finally admitted into Marjory Stoneman Douglas High School. Within a month he posted on Instagram a desire to shoot up the school. Early in his junior year he was suspended for fighting and reported to the state for evaluation after intentionally cutting his arms on the social media site Snapchat. A few months later he assaulted another student and was suspended from the school. A few weeks later he purchased one of the guns he would use the following year in the attack.

Ten months later his mother died of pneumonia, leaving him and his younger brother to go stay with friends, but Cruz's aggression quickly resulted in the family kicking him out. In a 9-1-1 call the family noted a collection of guns Cruz kept at a friend's house and his claims he was going to shoot someone.

For the final few months before the shooting, another family took him in, they reported no problems with him, he even got a job at Dollar Tree.

Between September 2017 and the month before the shooting there were multiple calls to law enforcement, including the FBI, that Cruz was making claims online of wanting to be a mass shooter, and making threats against people, in some cases reportedly putting guns to their heads. This should have triggered a response, but there was no follow-up.

On the day of the shooting, the first staff to see him

approaching the school with a backpack and rifle case should have signaled an alert and triggered a lockdown. The armed security at the school never approached Cruz and never entered the building even as shots could be heard inside.

Cruz's obsession with violence and guns should have been a red flag to be more aggressively treated. His mother should have initiated at least a short period of in-patient treatment.

Every system put in place to identify and interrupt a mass shooter failed in this case. Every point at which the progression could have been interrupted was missed, and this is a key concern when we talk about any system to either identify shooters before the attack or securing schools against attack.

School security becomes a hot topic after each shooting, especially when safeguards do not seem to work. Let's address it. First a caveat. Before we become terrified and close all public schools for the safety of our children, we need to keep in mind that school shootings resulting in injury or death are statistically rare but get massive media attention when they happen. This does not mean we should ignore them, but most schools will never experience a fatal mass shooting event. More children die each year in car accidents, or in the home, than in schools.

When there has been a publicized school shooting, the general public jumps toward "bucket" solutions, meaning oversimplified solutions that might or might not solve part of the problem, but are never a broad solution. Often the public will get on board with security measures which are already in place, such as demanding armed security or locked doors during school hours when the location of a recent shooting already had those measures in place.

The other concern is that most school shooters are current or former students of the school or the district, meaning they have access to the school and are aware of the security measures that are in place and can consider those measures when planning an attack. Unfortunately, statistics do not show any threat difference in schools with or without armed security, in fact, given that the majority of school shooters intend to end their own lives, the presence of armed security might attract them (Peterson, Densley & Erickson, 2020).

On May 18, 2018, 17-year-old Dimitrios Pagourtzis, a student at Santa Fe High School in Santa Fe, Texas, opened fire on a class in the school's art complex, killing 10 and wounding 17 before finally surrendering to police. Pagourtzis is a classic case of an intended murder/suicide mass shooting. He ultimately did not take his own life, but that was his intent. As police attempted to get him to surrender, he exchanged fire with them hoping to be shot; in the end he gave up. He had no history of mental health problems or violent behavior; his primary issue seemed to be depression, increasing suicidal ideation, and anger toward some students for rejecting and bullying him.

I mention this case because of what Pagourtzis did after firing the initial shots in the classroom. He knew there were two police officers assigned as armed security for the school, so he went out into the hallway, took a defensive position near the wall, and pointed his shotgun at the corner where the officers would emerge. The officers reacted exactly as they had been trained; they did everything right. They moved quickly but cautiously toward the sound of the shooting, and cautiously approached the corner of the hallway. The problem is, there is no way (outside of the cartoon physics in action movies) to get around that corner and target the shooter when the shooter is already there, weapon pointed, finger on the trigger, and using a weapon that does not require precise aim. As soon as the first officer made a move and Pagourtzis saw motion coming from around the corner, he pulled the trigger. The officer's arm was nearly blown off. He never had a chance to see the shooter. His partner did the only thing he could do, pulled his partner back, took his own defensive position in case the shooter came around the corner, then pulled back to get his partner medical aid.

There is sometimes talk of having a single school entrance with metal detectors. In the case of Santa Fe would that have stopped the shooter? Yes and no. He would not have made it into the school with his weapons, but he would not have needed to because the bottleneck created by the single entrance and the metal detector would have created a pool of targets outside the school greater than what he had in a single classroom. And it would have created the worst possible environment for armed security to get a clear line-of-sight shot at the shooter. Keep in mind, security does not want to take a chance of shooting innocent people, but the shooter does not care who they hit.

Columbine, Santa Fe, Parkland, all had armed security, none of them were able to stop the shooters. Sandy Hook Elementary closed and locked all doors once the students were in, but Adam Lanza simply shot through a glass panel near a locked door. Whatever security measures are put in place, shooters will find a way to work around them. That does not mean completely abandon the attempt to make schools safer, because anything that makes it harder for the shooter to carry out the plan, from accessing weapons to accessing the schools, makes it more likely they could be stopped before anyone is hurt. But no single solution is the "fix all" answer.

If you study school shootings, there is something else you might have noticed. The largest population centers in the country have the fewest mass-casualty school shootings. Most of the high-fatality shootings are in smaller rural communities. Santa Fe Texas had a population of less than 14,000. The Monday after the shooting there were arrests in four other communities in the area for students bringing weapons to school. Communities such as Friendswood (population 40,000), Cleveland Texas (population 8,000), Huffman (population 12,000), and Texas City (population 50,000). Newtown Connecticut, home of Sandy Hook Elementary had a population of 27,000. Parkland Florida had a population of 32,000. Of the ten deadliest school shootings in U.S. history, only one was in a community of over 100,000 (The Stockton school yard shooting in 1989).

Why smaller communities? And why are copycats nationwide more common after shootings in rural communities? The very traits that make small communities feel more supportive and personal can also make them feel more isolating and condemning. The most common school shooters are rural white teenage boys, who can easily feel a sense of connection to other rural white teenage boys regardless of where they live, unlike people in cities who do not feel the same sense of connection to people in other cities, or even people in their own cities. Thus, one rural shooter can be the tipping point for other potential rural shooters anywhere in the country.

In a smaller community a teen who feels outcast or bullied does not just feel it from peers, they feel it from the entire community. That sense of "everyone knows everyone else's business," especially communities with a single high school, can create an exaggerated sense that the whole world is against you, whereas in a larger community it is easier to find a niche, or find anonymity where there is not the same feeling of being judged.

In these cases, an attack on the school is not just an attack on students and staff, it is a revenge attack on the community itself. In 1927 when Andrew Kehoe blew up half the elementary school in Bath Township in Michigan, his target was not the 38 children who died, it was the school district, the community, and its leadership.

This is the danger of the Incel online community. They are individuals socially isolated in their real-world environment who find a supportive niche online who share their fantasies of real-world revenge and violence. Others in their online environment can fuel the temptation without any personal repercussion. Incel environments are particularly toxic because they are motivated by externalizing blame for the consequences of the individual's behavior; allowing them to perceive themselves as victims. An individual will enter one of these environments with a specific target of hostility but quickly be indoctrinated into hatred toward other demographics. How to address the growth of this population is problematic because it involves exaggerated expectations of traditional gender norms, frequently reinforced stereotypes, and the debate over "free speech" versus "dangerous speech" online.

Finally, let's address why school and mass shootings have increased in frequency, and more disturbing, increased in death-toll since the 1980s. For this we blend psychology and sociology and look back to the earlier chapter on the impact of media. In a nutshell, the cultural socialization and attitude toward guns has gradually changed. Partly due to media, and partly due to opportunistic politics using guns and gun ownership as a political tool.

If you grew up prior to the 1970s, especially if you grew up in a rural community, guns were probably very commonplace, but there was little talk of them representing rights, or the Second Amendment, or being necessary to protect you from the government. They were simply an appliance. Most gun-owning households would include a pistol, hunting rifles, and probably a shotgun. Maybe Old Man Chet who lived outside of town had an old WWII or Korean War era machine gun he lifted as a souvenir, and maybe a few people had semi-automatic rifles, but those weapons were more a novelty than a necessity. They had not been elevated to the glamourized status they have among gun enthusiasts today.

What happened to start the public obsession with semi-automatic weapons and guns in general? It was not shootings, or politicians threatening to take guns, it was the action movies of the late 70's into the 80's and 90's. Movies that glamourized the weapons and attached them to measures of masculinity. In some circles a simple and practical .22 caliber weapon became perceived as a weapon for "women and children." A "real man" had a higher caliber weapon, and an automatic or semiautomatic weapon became the ultimate in externalized displays of masculinity. What was once a novelty started to become more popular with typical gun owners. In young people they more frequently became the first choice when purchasing their own weapons. The public did not become concerned about the increase in the volume of these weapons until the Stockton schoolyard shooting in 1989, which was a big catalyst leading to the ten-year assault weapons ban from 1994 to 2004.

The ban was the second part of the progression. It politicized the weapons and cemented them as a representation of Second Amendment rights. Once politicians realized they could get votes and money by making either gun rights or gun control central to their platforms the race was on to scare the public on both sides. The ban did not take guns away from anyone, nor prevented anyone from purchasing them from private owners, it simply prevented manufacturers from selling them to the public. The rationale at the time was "There are enough of those weapons already in circulation for anyone who might want one, there is no need to flood the country with more." As you can imagine, in the hands of private owners, the value of the weapons escalated.

There was disagreement about whether the ban did anything while it was in place, but one thing was undeniable: It did something when it expired in 2004. The popularity of the weapons skyrocketed during the ban, and when it expired, sales took off. A second surge in sales occurred in late 2008 and early 2009 after the election of Barack Obama and a Democratic majority in Congress. There was an assumption at the time that the new administration and congressional majority would reinstate the ban.

It should be no surprise that the previously banned weapons became more common in both mass and school shootings after the ban was lifted than they had been before the ban was put in place. This added fuel to the gun control/gun rights debate.

I mentioned earlier that crime in general, including murder, began to decline in the mid-1990s and continued to decline until hitting a low in 2014 before starting to tick up again. This means the decline was happening during the first decade of the assault weapons ban but continued after the ban expired. Critics of the ban will point this out as evidence the ban had no effect on overall crime, which is true. But it did influence the number of high-profile, high fatality shooting events involving the banned weapons, with fewer during the decade of the ban, and a significant increase in the decade after the ban. Once the weapons were once again available in shops and stores, shooters did not have to make the effort to seek them out through private owners or illegal channels.

There were two factors converging: Availability, and glorification of the weapons as an easy "man card" for gender-insecure males. But another factor had been slowly evolving during and after the ban: An increasing negative perception by the non-gun-owning public of both guns and gun owners.

This next statement is going to seem counterintuitive and ridiculous but stick with me for a minute. The greatest damage to public perception of guns and gun owners did not come from gun control advocates, it came from the actions and responses of the National Rifle Association (NRA) to mass and school shootings and their decision to align themselves with the politicizing of the gun issue and attract politicians to their cause through lobbying and campaign donations.

How could this be? The criticisms of the assault weapons ban ranged from the practical (banning the weapons was a stunt to appease gun control advocates because the use of those weapons in shootings were high profile but statistically rare) to the paranoid and ridiculous (the ban is the first step in the government taking away all guns so they can control the population). Fear and paranoia are the bread and butter of politicians looking for votes and money, so it was no surprise they would feed the irrational more than argue the rational.

The NRA did not just challenge gun laws that could take guns from people, it began challenging any law connected to guns even if the general public perceived them as "common sense" laws to make it harder for dangerous people to acquire guns. This started to move public perception of the NRA in the direction of an extreme advocacy group, similar to how the public perceives PETA (People for the Ethical Treatment of Animals) and Greenpeace.

At the same time, each highly publicized mass or school shooting was met immediately by defense of the weapon. Although the NRA itself began to back away from this tactic, its supporters in mass media and social media did not.

Imagine it this way: If someone received a call that a loved one had been in a car accident, and their first question was "is the car okay?" You would probably have a very negative impression of them. This is how the general public started to view the quick defense of weapons after a shooting. Yes, the immediate emotional response after a high-fatality mass shooting, especially at a school, is anger toward both the shooter and the weapon, and immediate calls to ban such weapons, but it is not the time for gun rights advocates to add their voices. The smarter option would be to let the strong emotions around the event play out and save the defense until the politicians are starting to propose legislation.

And let's anchor one point in reality: The Second Amendment is part of the Constitution; it cannot be eliminated by simply passing a law or issuing an executive order. To truly get rid of it, such as deciding to turn gun rights to the individual states instead of a constitutional amendment, would require passing a new amendment abolishing it, and if that passed it would then have to be ratified by at least 38 of the 50 states. Not hard to see how in the current environment such an amendment would have little chance of passing or being ratified.

As we leave this chapter you probably noticed there were two very deadly and high-profile mass shootings I did not cover. The Pulse Nightclub shooting in June 2016 where Omar Mateen killed 49 people and injured 53 before being killed in a shootout with police, and the 2017 Las Vegas shooting, where Stephen Paddock opened fire on concert goers from a nearby hotel window, killing 60 and injuring 411 (with over 300 more injured trying to escape) before killing himself as police were attempting to enter his room. In both cases there was not enough solid, confirmed evidence to determine motive, or to track a progression leading to the shootings. In the case of Paddock, the best we can determine is alcoholism and escalating financial problems. In the case of Mateen the common theory is a hate crime and affiliation with international terrorist organizations, but if you want to spread "terror" in the U.S. it is unlikely you would target a marginalized group who are already a target of hostility within their own country. Other accounts suggest Mateen was a regular patron at the club and the killings might have been a way to exact revenge for romantic rejections or to cover his own homosexual leanings. Again, too much of the evidence is speculation, and many of the puzzle pieces do not fit.

We have set the stage for our final chapter; the one you have been waiting for: Serial Killers.

Chapter Eight

Serial Killers

First off, I understand the most likely audience for this book, so this chapter might not be as satisfying as you hope. Entire books have been written about the individual cases I am about to mention and the behavioral and neurological factors found most often in people who become serial killers. Most of these books emphasize how killers are different from us, but I am going to take a different angle and look at how they often start out just like us. Hopefully in this last chapter I can add a few new pieces to the puzzle of understanding serial killers.

We start with a technicality of definition. There is no global "profile of a serial killer." Serial Killer is a general term referring to number of victims over a period of time (Newton, 2006). Profiling begins as we look at categories based on physical patterns of the crime (organized, disorganized, and mixed), and categories based on motivation for the crime (power/control, mission-oriented, visionary, hedonistic, etc.). Keep in mind, our profiling data comes from studying the people who have been caught. Does that mean the people who have not been caught might not fit the profile and that's why they have not been caught? We always need to stay aware of the possible impact of the data we do not have, and not get overconfident in the data we do have.

We also need to address some terms that often get thrown around carelessly; psychopath and sociopath. Because these are not clinical terms (they are not in the DSM 5) you will find many variations in definition, including people who use the terms interchangeably. There is nothing wrong with these varieties of definition so long as people are clear which definitions they are using, so for our purposes a psychopath is someone who lacks empathy, cares little, if at all, about the impact they have on others, is very controlled and proactive, planning their behavior for personal gain and often described as "cold hearted." Sociopath is defined most simply as a psychopath who was raised in an environment of abuse or emotional neglect. Rather than controlled and calculating they are very impulsive and reactionary, often described as "hot headed." A psychopath can blend in and appear mostly normal, but a sociopath tends to stand out very quickly. For example, you are at a party, and I send in a psychopath and a sociopath with instructions to try to get you to voluntarily leave the party with them. The sociopath will give you bad vibes, you'll likely be wary of them and possibly even perceive them as a potential threat. But you are likely to leave with the psychopath because they might feel like the safest person in the room. When people say they could spot a psychopath because "you can see it in their eyes" they are talking about a sociopath.

If a psychopath lacks empathy and has an impaired ability to make emotion-based connections with others, why are they often considered "charming" and can so easily and effectively manipulate people? It comes down to how the brain of a neurotypical person "reads" the emotions of others.

Facial expressions and body language associated with genuine outward displays of emotion are not learned, they are hardwired into us. The only time we might try to "learn" them is when we are learning to fake them. For example, regardless of time or culture happiness creates a specific observable response, as does sadness, anger, disgust, etc. This means when you are in a conversation with another person your brain is unconsciously recognizing their facial expressions and body language as representing specific emotions (your brain knows what emotion you would be experiencing if you were displaying the same expression), this causes your brain to produce an echo of that same emotion, causing you to echo the same facial expressions and body language. We are not consciously aware of this, but this is thought to be the neural and motor mechanisms which give us an "intuitive" sense that a person is being genuine, or not. For example, when someone is faking a response, such as an exaggerated frown in response to your display of a low mood, your brain interprets it as superficial and fake, possibly to the point of being insulting. Faked facial expressions are almost always too exaggerated, and the expressions can change either too rapidly or be maintained for too long compared to natural expressions. Unless you are startled into a new emotion, your facial expressions do not shift rapidly, they form and recede in waves.

The result of all this is that when someone is genuinely echoing our facial expressions and body language, we tend to find them more likeable.

Psychopaths possess this same mechanism of echoing facial expression and body language, but they seem to lack the neural connections which associate the expressions with emotions, and they do it regardless of how intently they are listening to you. The eyes are seeing it, the motor cortex spontaneously echoes it creating the visible display which generates an impression in the other person that the psychopath is interested and maybe even compassionate. The only visible difference is that because the psychopath is not experiencing the emotion, the expression can shift rapidly, such as when moving from one conversation to another.

There is another issue related to the problem of connecting emotion to physical display, a problem not limited to psychopath and sociopath. Because they seem to have a disconnect in emotional interpretation when interacting with others, they also have difficulty understanding when their behavior is causing a reaction in someone else, therefore, they might see the reaction as unwarranted or unfair. For example, if I am having an argument with someone, and I have been throwing verbal zingers at them, and they throw one back; I understand this is in the context of our argument and my behavior is eliciting this behavior from them. But if my ability to socially read the other person is impaired, I might have a very poor perception of how my words are impacting them, and therefore feel like their zinger came out of nowhere and is unfair. This is going to be especially true in the impulsive and emotionally volatile reactions of sociopaths.

I mentioned that psychopath and sociopath are descriptors, based heavily on observable behavior, but are not clinically defined in the DSM 5, yet there are often assumptions of what the equivalent is within the DSM. Most often there is an assumption that psychopaths and sociopaths by default would meet the criteria for Antisocial Personality Disorder, but this is not necessarily true. The criteria for psychopathy can be found across other personality disorders as well including Borderline, Narcissistic, and Histrionic (Abdalla-Filho & Völlm, 2020).

Keep in mind, of those we would label as "psychopathic" we often assume they intentionally cause harm to people. The majority of people who fit the criteria never become killers; they gravitate toward careers which fit their traits, and generally do not *intentionally* hurt people, they hurt people because they are unaware of how their traits, words, and behavior impact those around them. This is common with all the personality disorders I mentioned.

Right now, you might be wondering about the parallel between the traits I have mentioned and autism spectrum. That is a hot topic and quite controversial but also understandable. I will address that in a specific example later in the chapter.

At the beginning of the chapter I mentioned categories of serial killer based on the physical characteristics of the crime, and categories based on motivation. We need some brief definitions before we start tossing those words around in describing specific killers.

Before defining "organized" and "disorganized," I need to emphasize that these are not mutually exclusive categories; it is not all one or the other. Think of them as anchor points at the opposite ends of a spectrum; different pieces of evidence will lean the scene in one direction or the other, with a range within the middle we would call "mixed."

Organized usually reflects premeditation, planning, and choosing a specific victim or, if the victim is random, preplanning of what will be done to the victim. An organized killer will often take more time with the victim both before and after death. They are more likely to use restraints, and more likely to transport the body to a predetermined disposal location. As far as personal characteristics they are likely to have a very controlled mood during the crime, be of average or above-average intelligence (not genius level as often portrayed in media), relatively socially skilled, and will watch the news for reports of what they have done. As far as childhood influence, the most common trends focus on the father. If the father is present he likely had consistent work, meaning a relatively stable financial environment, but discipline was inconsistent, meaning as a child the person could not predict the consequences of their behavior, but when punishment occurred it was less likely to be harsh.

The most popular example of an organized killer is Ted Bundy, but we will see he had several disorganized traits as well and there is reason to suspect he might have committed disorganized murders which were never connected to him because they did not fit his usual pattern. John Wayne Gacy and Dennis Rader (BTK killer) would be other examples.

Disorganized, as you would expect, is the opposite. Because they are more impulsive and lack emotional control the killings are likely to be spontaneous, with no pre-planning, and the victims are whoever is around at the moment. Violence is sudden, the body is left at the scene and often in view, and they will frequently leave a weapon behind. Usually of below-average intelligence and socially awkward, they will be in an agitated mood during the crime and show little interest in news reports of their crimes. In childhood, if a father was present, he was chronically unemployed or in a financially poor or unstable job. Punishment would have been consistent and harsh, creating resentment and a suppressed need to lash out. They are more likely to have been physically or sexually abused as children.

Richard Chase, the "Vampire of Sacramento" would be an example of disorganized killer, as would Tommy Lynn Sells, the "Psychokiller Drifter."

In defining the different motivations, we must also be cautious in thinking of a single killer as "all or nothing" in one of these categories. There can be a mix, and over time the motivation might evolve from one category to another. Richard Kuklinski (the "ice man"), started as a power/control killer and evolved later more toward mission oriented.

Visionary is the rarest of the serial killer motivations. They are motivated by mental illness, quite often delusions or hallucinations. The defining characteristic is a psychotic break from reality. Rare because mental illness-related murder is a minority of all murders anyway, but also because most killers with this motivation will fall in the disorganized category, therefore they will be impulsive, emotion-driven, and sloppy. Some will be captured before they fit the criteria for "serial killer."

A frequent example, which turned out to be a hoax, was David Berkowitz, the "Son of Sam" killer who claimed a dog instructed him to carry out the killings (he later claimed he made up that story).

A classic example is Herbert Mullin, the California serial killer who killed 13 people between October 1972 and February 1973. Mullin had experienced escalating symptoms of schizophrenia from his late teens into his early twenties, resulting in five brief commitments to mental health facilities in just a few years. Fueling this progression was his use of LSD (never a good choice for someone with a history of psychotic symptoms). Mullin believed that blood sacrifice, in the form of U.S. troop deaths in Vietnam, was preventing a catastrophic earthquake in California. But in 1972 the U.S. began large pullouts of troops, relying more on air than ground attacks, which resulted in a drastic drop in the number of troop deaths. Mullin thought he was receiving telepathic messages telling him to start making sacrifices to prevent the inevitable catastrophe. His killings were very impulsive and random. A group of teenagers camping, a woman and her family who answered the door when Mullin accidentally went to the wrong address trying to locate an old high school teammate, a Catholic priest in a confessional box, and his final victim, a man out in his yard gardening, who Mullin spotted as he was driving by. Mullin shot him in broad daylight, in full view of neighbors (who noted his license plate), then casually drove away. Police arrested him for that murder but did not immediately connect him to the other killings because the patterns, weapons, and victim demographics varied so much. They might never have connected the cases if Mullin had not voluntarily confessed to all of them. A classic example of both visionary and disorganized.

Mission-oriented have a specific goal which they use as justification for killing. Usually this means targeting groups they consider "inferior" or "unworthy." Frequent targets are marginalized or vulnerable groups. But do they really believe they are making the world a better place? Or are they just using this as a rationalization to kill? If they have a true dislike for a group and feel the group is a burden on society, they might truly believe killing them is a benefit to society. Some might feel the homeless are a burden and it helps society as well as being a merciful end to the perceived miserable life of the homeless person (an altruistic mission-oriented, organized serial killer?). They could perceive sex industry workers as lowering the moral standards of a community and attracting drugs and crime, therefore killing them is doing a service. The homeless and sex industry workers specifically make easy targets who are less likely to be missed right away and even when discovered will attract less public interest or investigative energy. Both of those populations can be very transient, so someone disappearing is not uncommon.

But "helping society" could also be an attempt to rationally justify irrational drives; an attempt to think of themselves as noble rather than a monster. Gary Ridgway, the Green River Killer is sometimes thought of as mission oriented, but he more likely fits the lust subset of our next category:

Hedonistic killers derive pleasure from killing. They chase the thrill. For them killing can become an addiction, and like the effects of a substance the act of killing can produce an addictive rush. Hedonistic is divided into three subtypes: Lust, Thrill, and Comfort.

Lust killers are primarily driven by sex. The roots of this begin in sexual fantasy, specifically fantasies of domination and control, which over time become associated with aggression; causing aggression itself to become sexually arousing.

Like an addiction, lust killers will habituate to the rush, and over time will start to seek it out more frequently. They are more likely to use torture to extend their time with the victim before killing them. Jeffrey Dahmer is considered a classic example of a lust killer, and as I mentioned previously, Gary Ridgway is also a fit for this category.

Thrill killers are also driven by the rush they get from killing, but there is no sexual aspect to it. They thrive on the pain and terror they elicit from their victims. All of these categories can potentially evolve into thrill killers.

Comfort killers are seeking personal gain connected to material goods or lifestyle. Their victims are most commonly family members or acquaintances. They will go long periods of time between kills in order to avoid suspicion. The "black widow" type killer, who kills romantic partners for insurance or inheritance is a comfort killer.

Power/Control killers share several of the traits of other categories, but their motivation is exclusively dominating the victim. When they commit sexual assault, it is motivated by control or punishment rather than sexual urges.

As I mentioned earlier, and will mention again as I describe specific cases, these types are not necessarily permanent in an individual. There can be a primary motivation fueling the first murder, but the experience of the killings can cause a change in motivation. This is likely the reason some victims will never be connected to their killer because the majority of the killer's victims follow a specific pattern, while earlier victims might have been of a different demographic or presented as a different profile.

Cognitive Progression to serial murder.

In an earlier chapter I talked about common cognitive traits and thinking patterns which can escalate over time and lead to the risk of murder. Are there similar traits that can lead someone to becoming a serial killer? Yes. But first I must address the question "Are serial killers made, or are they born?" Meaning does environment create them or is it a neurological difference they have from birth? The answer is either or both, but neither are guaranteed to produce a killer. Research that claims to find unique neurology to killers will usually implicate the amygdala (emotional regulation) and its interaction with the frontal lobes (impulse control, decision making, and perception of consequence). Such research is not wrong in that killers have these neurological traits, but these traits are common in the "non killer" population as well. We find similar patterns common in many of the personality disorders as well as in Autism Spectrum Disorder (ASD) and Attention Deficit/Hyperactivity Disorder (ADHD) as well as in chronic long-term sufferers of Post-Traumatic Stress Disorder (PTSD). Is it a combination of this neurological foundation with environmental factors? Again, we can find consistency in killers having difficult or abusive childhoods leading to violent fantasy which can progress to violent behavior, but these factors are also, unfortunately, common in the non-killer general population. So, is it a perfect storm of factors which lead to serial killing? Very likely. But let me address one frequent claim first: Some people are just born bad.

In the 1956 film "The Bad Seed" (LeRoy, 1956), Patty McCormack played a sweet eight-year-old girl who also happened to be murdering anyone who got in her way. This, despite having seemingly wonderful parents and a stable home environment. This film reflected, and reinforced, the belief that parents were not always responsible for kids turning out bad, sometimes they were just born that way. This approach has always been problematic because too often it was a smokescreen to hide abuse by parents. For decades, and still in some circles today, there was the idea that if a child was not responding to punishment, you escalate the punishment, making it harsher, and eventually they will learn. Does this work? No. Data has been building for decades showing that harsh punishment, even if it successfully corrects a target behavior, leads to resentment, rebellion, and aggression (Gershoff, 2002). And it is even worse if the child is in any way neurodivergent.

For punishment to work, the individual must associate the punishment with the behavior that elicited it, and to be truly effective the punishment must follow very closely in time to the behavior. This is why the generations raised on the "wait till your dad gets home" style of punishment more likely learned to fear dad than to learn proper behavior.

Now imagine you have a neurological divergence that makes it difficult to associate your behavior to the punishment, or to be able to control the behavior that elicited the punishment. You are either not going to understand why you are being punished, therefore resent it, or are unable to control the behavior and receive harsher punishment, creating a desire to lash out.

Kids in previous decades who today would be recognized as Autism Spectrum or ADHD were often labeled as "problem children" or "attitude problems" and too often the traditional solution was simply to escalate punishment until they got the hint. It would be no different than punishing someone in a wheelchair every time they refused to stand.

The flip side of this two-headed coin is emotional neglect. We assume aggression always comes from abuse, but it seems to also come from emotional and/or environmental neglect. A child raised in a financially supportive environment with parents who rarely ever punish them, and rarely ever interact with them or show them affection, is also likely to display aggression later in life. Harry Harlow's infamous "Nature of Love" study from 1958, more commonly known as "Harlow's Monkeys" was an example of this. He did many variations of this experiment but the best known is the "cloth mother/wire mother" variation in which an infant monkey, separated from its mother at birth and never allowed physical interaction with other monkeys, was given a choice of a soft warm mother-figure who did not provide nourishment, or a wire-frame mother who did provide nourishment. The infants spent most of their time on the comforting mother, and only enough time on the wire mother to feed. But there was another interesting observation (you can see this yourself if you look up videos of Harlow's experiments), when the two mothers were placed side-by-side the infant would cling to the soft mother and lean over to feed from the wire mother, and even though the artificial plastic faces of the two mothers were identical, the infant would aggressively scratch and bite at the face of the wire mother; the one providing food but no comfort.

Another fly in the ointment of "kids born bad" regarding serial killers is that many of them did not show signs of psychopathy in youth, at least not signs that were obvious enough to be indicators at the time. It is always easy in hindsight to go back and look at behavior and say "Oh, the signs were there," when at the time the signs did not stand out at all.

What about the infamous MacDonald Triad? Setting fires, bed-wetting, and animal cruelty. At one time these were thought to be predictive of adult predatory behavior if the behaviors continued into the teen years. Today they are more commonly seen as signs of physical or sexual abuse; the product of anxiety and suppressed anger which cannot be vented at the abuser(s).

Let's address Animal cruelty specifically. Does escalating cruelty to animals, especially killing them, represent a step toward being willing to kill humans? It depends on how the individual internally classifies the animal as a "life." Is a child who is stomping ants on the sidewalk showing signs of future psychopathy? What about a person who hunts for sport?

Here's a thought question you might have played with before. How big, complex, or relatable does a living creature have to be before we feel its life has value? We step on ants, smash spiders, swat flies, but of course those are insects. We consider insect lives to be less important and of little value. What about rodents? We use kill-traps and poison for mice and rats. Does that count as animal cruelty, or do they not count because they are "pest" animals? Someone who keeps rats as pets might consider rat traps and poisons to be animal cruelty. Would you feel the same putting traps or poisons out for rats as you would for squirrels? Aren't squirrels little more than rats with fluffy tails?

By the time we reach cats and dogs we are into culturally recognized "pet" categories. Mistreatment is considered cruelty, and there are laws protecting them from abuse.

As we come up the scale from small living things to larger living things, we assign greater value to their lives, unless they enter the category of food animal. One culture might view cows and pigs as food animals while another does not. One might view cats and dogs as food while another does not. Some eat insects while others find the thought disgusting. Cultures will frequently judge each other's "humanity" by the categories of their food animals.

We place a similar hierarchy on the value of human life. The closer someone is to us in relation, acquaintance, geography, or group identity, the more we feel it emotionally when something terrible happens to them. The image of the World Trade Center towers in New York being struck and collapsing on September 11, 2001 was more emotional for people living in Denver than for people living in Toronto, Canada, even though Toronto is geographically closer. The collective "U.S. Citizen" identity was more emotionally triggered, regardless of how far away they were, than people who identified as citizens of countries that were not targeted.

In times of war we feel bad for innocent citizens killed during military conflicts, but it is dependent on whether those people were citizens of allied countries or enemy countries. Western media gave much more coverage to displacement and deaths of Ukrainian citizens during the Russian invasion in 2022 than to the displacement and deaths of Iraqi citizens during the U.S. invasion in 2003. Which side you are on matters in how you interpret the value of life and whether you interpret deaths as "tragic" or as "collateral damage."

As painful as it is to admit it, the general public is not as moved by the deaths of people in lower socioeconomic statuses as they are of people in the middle class. The murder of a homeless person does not produce the same sympathy, media attention, or investigative response as the murder of someone in the middle class or higher. All else being equal, if the case of murdered six-year-old JonBenet Ramsey in 1996 had involved a poor family living in a single-wide mobile home it would not have received the same media attention or public interest.

As I mentioned in earlier chapters, if we subjectively feel that someone "deserved" it we care less about their death than the death of an innocent person. Serial killers possess these same hierarchies; the difference being the values they perceive exist along different points of the hierarchy than other people, and they include the additional trait of being able to actively bring about the death of a living being (you might not care about the death of a homeless person, but that does not mean you would murder a homeless person), yet much of the cognitive foundation necessary for them to make that leap is also present in most of us.

To go back to the question of hurting animals representing a progression toward hurting humans, the key factor is how the individual was socialized to perceive animals, and how their early environment socialized them to perceive a hierarchy of value in human lives. Some people are never introduced directly to the idea of animals as pets, only to the idea of animals as food or pests, so their lives have no value. Other children raised in such an environment might also be socialized to see certain categories of human as being near the spectrum of "animals" and therefore the thought of harming them is not the same as harming "valuable" humans. As we will see later, childhood can be a critical time in interrupting these perceptions to reduce the chance of a gradual tragic progression.

With these various factors and categories in mind, let's look at some specific cases and where they either fall into, or crossover, some of these types.

Gary Ridgway, the Green River Killer was eventually convicted of 49 murders committed between 1982 and 1998, but investigators believe he killed more than 70 during his active years. Ridgway claims he killed so many he lost count and probably forgot many. To this day there are unsolved cases which are likely connected to him, and bodies that have yet to be discovered, but he could not specifically recall them and/or there is not enough evidence to formally connect him. His nickname comes from the discovery of his first five victims along the Green River near Kent, Washington (a few minutes south of Seattle. Side note, the location where those bodies were found is now part of a golf course constructed by the city of Kent in 1989).

Ridgway is considered "organized" because of his planning and the tactics he used to avoid detection (disposing of bodies in clusters at dump sites knowing media would report police presence if they were discovered and dumping three bodies in Oregon so authorities might think he had moved, etc.). Some say he is "mission oriented" because he targeted sex workers, considering them "garbage," and therefore helping society by getting rid of them. He could also be a fit for "hedonistic/lust" because he sought them out for sex before killing them.

That last point is why he is not a good fit for mission oriented. "Cleaning society" of them was a convenient self-justification, but throughout his history he displayed a pattern of sex obsession. This combined with his habit of returning to his dump sites to have sex with the bodies puts him well into the "lust" subcategory of the hedonistic motivation.

A caution in trying to explain or understand a serial killer based on their own statements, especially if those statements have come after arrest but before conviction. They could be making up accounts or exaggerating specific life experiences in order to influence conviction and sentencing, especially if the death penalty is being considered. I earlier mentioned David Berkowitz, "Son of Sam" who likely created the story of a dog telling him to commit murders so he could plead insanity and receive a lighter sentence or commitment to a mental hospital rather than prison.

I mention this because some key points of Gary Ridgway's history, especially those which seem to point some blame toward his mother, come from Ridgway himself rather than from objective sources. I will rely here on the summaries resulting from the various official investigations into Ridgway (State of Washington vs. Gary Leon Ridgway, 2003), assuming they did their homework and because they interviewed as many people a possible connected to Ridgway.

For example, Ridgway claimed that when he was a teenager, he intentionally stabbed a small child (6 years old) just to feel what it was like to stab someone. He was never identified or apprehended in that case, but investigators were able to track down the victim (by that time in his 40s and living in California) to confirm the incident. Although only six years old at the time of the stabbing, the victim did not require any prompting by detectives to remember the incident and confirm what Ridgway had done, what he had said, and how he behaved afterward (laughing as he walked away). The stabbing had damaged the boy's liver, requiring surgery and several weeks recovery in the hospital. A short time afterward the family moved to California.

Ridgway, by his own admission, was a compulsive liar, and this is reflected in the prosecutor's summary as Ridgway changed stories several times, few if any of them fitting the facts of the case, before finally being truthful with his accounts. For example, he initially claimed no connection to the bodies found in the Portland Oregon area which had been connected to him, but later gave detailed accounts (which could only be known by the killer) of the victims, condition of the bodies, locations where he dumped them, and the timeline of events.

Ridgway was born in 1949 in Utah, the second of three children. His parents moved to the Seattle area (what is today the community of SeaTac) when he was eleven. This could be significant because relocating in the pre-teen years is frequently difficult due to leaving any existing peer groups and needing to start again as "the new kid." His mother was mostly a homemaker who sometimes worked part-time at a department store. Neighbors report her as having a temper, sometimes getting in loud shouting arguments with her spouse and possibly the children and being very controlling, especially with Gary. Some neighbors have said she dressed very provocatively for the time, in revealing tops and short skirts. Ridgway was a bedwetter in his early teens, but little is known about the timeline, whether it was present before the family moved or started afterward.

Ridgway was a middle child. Normally this is not significant, but his older brother was more successful and praised for being more intelligent (Ridgway's IQ was listed in the mid-80s; near a full standard deviation below average), while Ridgway was held back in high school, not graduating until he was 19. Ridgway's childhood behavior (hurting animals and bedwetting) seems a strong indicator he was victim of physical or sexual abuse in childhood. Reportedly, his mother would bathe him after a bedwetting episode and specifically wash his genitals, even in his early teen years. He recalls one instance when she was wearing nothing but a robe, and while washing his genitals her robe fell open revealing that she was naked underneath. He later described his feelings for his mother as being a combination of sexual attraction and a desire to hurt her. He describes forming violent fantasies during his early teens of killing her, in the ways he later killed his victims. These fantasies seemed to have been forming long before the incident in which he stabbed the young boy to "feel what it is like to stab someone." It would not be much of a stretch to think he was practicing with a vulnerable victim as an easy target to vent his desire to hurt his mother.

After high school Ridgway joined the Navy, and it was here he began seeking out sex workers to satisfy his growing sexual obsessions. He became angered when he would pick up sexually transmitted diseases from them, but continued seeking them out, even after leaving the Navy and during his marriages. It is important to note he blamed the sex workers for the STIs, not his own behavior in seeking them out and engaging in unprotected sex. He admits that sex was the primary driver, and the desire to kill was a parallel urge which grew over time.

In this way Ridgway is very similar to other serial killers. He describes homicide as a craving, like an addiction, and sometimes the craving felt satisfied and he could go a time without it. But it would build again until he was driven to satisfy it.

Ridgway is also an example of something much more common, the danger of connecting sexuality and violence to the point that violence itself becomes arousing. This is a progression which probably started with the fantasies about his mother. It was compounded by his anger over sex workers giving him STIs, and the affairs of his first wife, a short marriage between 1970 and 1972 while he was in the Navy. According to the Prosecutor's summary, Ridgway said his wife "became a whore" while he was overseas, having several affairs. Again, he judged her for stepping outside the marriage while not judging himself for doing the same. He married a second time in 1973. The second wife noticed a progression during their marriage toward aggressive and controlling sexual behavior, becoming more interested in bondage, and wanting to have sex outdoors (in several locations where he would later dispose of bodies). He also became very religious during this time, obsessively reading the Bible, weeping at sermons, preaching door-to-door, and insisting his wife strictly follow the teachings of their Pastor to the letter. It was never officially confirmed that Ridgway was committing murders during his second marriage, but his wife reports he would stay out late into the evening and come home muddy. Their marriage ended in 1981. The following year began the most prolific two years of his killing spree, killing at least 40 women.

Does religious obsession seem to conflict with murdering sex workers? Not at all. By the end of his second marriage he had a well-established pattern of externalizing blame rather than being personally accountable for his actions. It is not hard to imagine the cognitive defense of absolving his sin of sex by killing the sex worker. Much like anyone guilty of something they label as morally wrong will go over-the-top in demonizing and condemning others who engage in the same behavior. The cognitive defense being "Yes, I do it, but by punishing or condemning others I am making up for my own behavior."

Why were the escalating violent and sexual fantasies not a threat to his wife? They almost were. By his own admission, Ridgway had fantasies about killing his wife near the end of their marriage; the only thing that prevented it was the awareness that he would be the primary suspect. In interviews with detectives Ridgway placed part of the blame for his crimes on his second wife not being a good partner, saying he might not have killed so many people if he had a better wife. Aside from how he would define "better wife" his statement by itself might be true given the statistics; between his divorce in 1981 and his third marriage in 1988 he is known to have killed at least 45 women. During his third marriage (which lasted until after his arrest in 2001) he is only known to have killed three. In fact, most of his killings were in 1982 and 1983. In 1984 he began dating and was briefly engaged; he is only known to have killed two women that year. The following year he met the woman who would later become his third wife, between the time they started dating and the day they were married Ridgway is only confirmed to have killed one person. If he was driven by an urge to kill, that urge seemed to be controlled by the presence of a stabilizing relationship.

You're probably wondering, what kind of relationship would be "stabilizing" for someone with Ridgway's urges? A pattern that is quite common: A spouse who is "in control" in most aspects of the relationship, possibly even "controlling," but allows the partner to be dominant and controlling in the sexual side of the relationship.

Let's look at the progression of Gary Ridgway and whether killing was inevitable or preventable. Given the right interventions at the right time could he have lived a relatively normal life and never become a murderer? Probably. We have already mentioned one, a romantic partner who could both control but at the same time allow relatively safe venting of his urges. But what about earlier? The childhood and early teen years when these tendencies seemed to first form and start growing?

It's always dangerous to imply details from general accounts, such as Ridgway's childhood, but if we take the stabbing of the child as the first outward sign of Ridgway's violence, one directed at a male child, not an adult woman, it gives us the ability to combine this with the bedwetting, dominant mother, and attachment to mother, to say there were triggers in childhood that could have been avoided.

Many of the murderers I have covered in this book, especially the white, heterosexual males, have a weak foundation of identity caused by gender insecurity. This is a byproduct of gender socialization and cultural messaging through media that men are supposed to be powerful, in control, live by their own rules, and be providers and protectors of women. "Protector" however, is often interpreted as meaning dominating and controlling more than providing and protecting. That would be fine if the natural world worked that way, but women are far more capable than the restrictive norms society tries to impose on them. How many households, do you suspect, played the traditional role of the father being in control, and the primary disciplinarian, but in reality it was the mother who was the real power, the one who really ran the show, and the one who could cause the greatest disruption in the household if you angered her? If you think hard about it, probably a lot. When we establish women as the primary caregivers and homemakers then women are the frontline power in the environment. In the case of Ridgway, he had a dominating, possibly abusive mother in a world where the norms told him he should dominate women. In other words, he was personally dominated by women while at the same time wanting to control them due to resentment over the control they had. Why can I draw such a specific description from the stories of his childhood? Because of growing aggression (stabbing the child) and seeking out sex workers as soon as he moved from home (when he joined the Navy). The pattern and frequency of Ridgway's killing correlated to the degree that a romantic relationship could control him. Sex workers became both the outlet of control and the outlet for aggression. This same pattern is present in another group we have mentioned several times: Incels (Involuntary Celibates), Ted Bundy is often viewed as an incel killer. In other words, they externalize blame for their romantic failures onto others, a trait we have already determined was present in Gary Ridgway.

It is disconcerting to think that there are thousands of potential serial and mass killers out there right now, who are only held in check by the presence of a strong relationship with a partner, but Gary Ridgway's patterns seem to suggest this is possible.

Do we only see these patterns in such extremes? Or are there more common examples that can lead to the same pattern? There are. A statement usually meant more as manipulation than real threat, but you probably recognize it; "If you leave me, I'll kill myself." I'm not saying such a person will suddenly turn into a mass or serial killer, but the willingness to make such a statement, and possibly really feel it, is moving them into a dangerous cognitive neighborhood; the cognitions found in murder/suicide. The next step is "If I can't have you, no one can."

Of course, not all Incels turn into killers, not everyone who had dominating, or abusive caregivers becomes a killer, not everyone who experiences head trauma becomes a killer. There is a Venn diagram of influences that overlap.

Let's add into this mix the personality dimensions of the "Dark Tetrad" which are found frequently in male customers of sex workers (Davis, Vaillancourt & Arnocky, 2020). The Dark Tetrad is an unfortunate combination of narcissism, Machiavellianism, psychopathy, and sadism. In a nutshell someone who is ego-centric, manipulative, callous, and enjoys the suffering of others. The complete stereotype of serial killer. Of course, not everyone with this combination is going to be a killer, it is not hard to imagine how these traits could be beneficial in the corporate world, but it is also not hard to imagine how dangerous it can be if this template is combined with the other factors we have already covered.

Which brings us back to the "born bad" question and whether anything can be done to identify and correct these traits early in childhood or the teen years. Can early intervention help any of the serial killers we are covering in this chapter, especially when the criteria for psychopathy are present?

As with any disorder that is considered persistent and lifelong the answer is it cannot be cured, but it likely can be managed. Meaning we cannot get rid of the roots, but we can give people the tools to interrupt and replace the behavior. There are multiple problems in identifying and treating these traits early in childhood, such as identifying whether a problematic trait will be enduring versus being a phase they will "grow out of." Most young children fit the criteria for psychopath because they are still very ego-centric and have not yet learned to understand the perspective of others. These are traits we expect to diminish with age. This is also why the personality disorders in the DSM should not be diagnosed prior to adulthood; many of the "symptoms" can be stages of maturation. For example, it might be disturbing, but not unexpected, to see two boys fighting in the hallway of a middle school, but seeing two adults fighting in the hallway of a University would be considered much more unusual because it is a behavior they should have grown out of by that time.

There is an empirically supported treatment method for psychopathy that might give us a clue into how parents can inadvertently cause an escalation in psychopathic behavior without realizing it. Simply put, individuals with psychopathic traits do not respond to punishment. Rather than connecting it to their behavior, they externalize it onto the punisher, creating resentment and anger. They do, however, respond to reinforcement/reward (Hawes & Dadds, 2005). No, this does not mean reward them for bad behavior, it means reinforce the positive behavior with reward, and correct the negative behavior by instructing them what alternative behavior would have generated reward. The traits associated with the Dark Tetrad are heavily reward-driven, so it makes sense they would respond well to any reward. Leaving bad behavior unchecked leads to a perceived sense of reward for getting away with bad behavior.

Can you see the problem when we try to apply this model to "traditional" forms of parental discipline? It takes work to watch for positive behavior and reward it, it takes much less effort to react to bad behavior and punish it, and if the punishment does not work then escalate the punishment until it does work, and if escalating punishment does not work, then the kid is simply a "bad seed."

Gary Ridgway is not alone as a serial killer with an uninterrupted series of contributing factors which left him spiraling unchecked toward murder, another is the Ice Man.

Richard Kuklinski did not earn the "Ice Man" nickname because he was a cold-blooded killer, but because in his later career he would freeze some of his victims, store them for a time, then later dump them to throw off police in determining time of death. One of his victims was unfortunately discovered too soon after being dumped and upon autopsy it was discovered his internal organs were still frozen.

Kuklinski was born in New Jersey in 1935 to Polish immigrant parents. His father was described as a violent alcoholic who left the family when Richard was five years old after beating one of Richard's older siblings to death and reporting it as an accident. He would sometimes return briefly, each visit resulting in violent arguments with his wife and beating the children. Kuklinski's mother worked in a meat processing plant. Her parenting mantra was strict religious guidance (Kuklinski was a choir boy in the church) and harsh discipline. Kuklinski described her as "poison" and said she destroyed everything she touched (The Iceman, 2004).

You can already see a very poor foundation being formed. Outward passivity as a result of abuse and inner rage looking to vent led to Kuklinski being picked on and often assaulted by local teen gangs, until one day, when Kuklinski was 13, he had enough. He took a wooden dowel from a closet and beat a gang leader to death, then pursued the others and severely beat them. He disposed of the body by pulling out the teeth and cutting off the fingertips to limit identification and dumped the body off a bridge. It was never recovered. After that incident he felt empowered, the rage came forward, and he became known as someone with a quick, hot temper rather than a passive victim.

You can already see how upbringing set the stage and the environment provided the plot. Kuklinski escaped the physical abuse of his family, but he did not escape the beatdown to his self-perception. He did not perceive himself as someone who could go to school and learn a trade, or in general work any kind of regular job. He sought work in the underworld. One of his first jobs was making pirated copies of movies, and from there pirated copies of porn which was distributed by local organized crime. This was his foot in the door to be exposed to the more violent side of the underworld. He essentially became a hit man, and later branched out on his own.

This is one of the tragedies of Kuklinski, who as a young man felt he could not learn a trade or work in a legitimate job. He demonstrated a skill for business when he ventured out on his own. Something which could have been channeled earlier in life into a legitimate career.

Ultimately, he would be charged for five murders, but likely committed far more.

Some of the professionals who have studied him dismiss many of his claims as fictionalized bragging, exaggeration, or flat out lying just to mess with the people interviewing him, but some of his accounts were detailed and consistent enough upon retelling that they were probably true.

Kuklinski fits the definition of "serial killer" because he had multiple victims over an extended period of time, and each victim was a singular event, but he does not fit most of the models because he was doing it as part of his job. He did not hunt victims to satisfy a homicidal urge. He fits the "Comfort" type of serial killer because he did it for personal gain.

There is a parallel here between the way Kuklinski could rationalize killing and the way a soldier can rationalize it: It's a job, and the person(s) have done something, threaten to do something, or represent a group that deserves it. Kuklinski did not kill completely "innocent" people. He killed people involved in organized crime, or who were trying to engage in crimes for profit. Not hard to rationalize that the victim's actions or intent remove them from the category of "innocent" and put them into a category where their life has less value and their death is justified.

Kuklinski is also a crossover because outside of his murders for profit there were a handful, such as his first murder, which fit the criteria for rage killing, when people would anger him enough to set him off. Again, in a blind rage scenario the brain perceives the victim as deserving it in that moment. Statistically, a much more common motivation for murder.

Given that he was raised in such a strict religious environment, did he completely reject it, or did he somehow rationalize his killings within a religious context? This one is not hard to answer. As mentioned earlier, most of the people he killed were criminals. Sinners. The religious template itself added to his belief that the victims deserved it because of who they were and what they were doing.

It might sound like I am trying to forgive Kuklinski's actions or create sympathy for him. Not at all. Once the choices are made you are responsible for your choices and your actions. The point here is simply to show how choices at key points in his life could have been different; how he could have been guided in a different direction, but such guidance was absent. And how, other than the blanket label of "evil" he could justify his actions in a way which made them feel acceptable.

Kuklinski died in prison on March 5, 2006 from cardiac arrest resulting from heart disease.

Of everyone we cover in this chapter, no one is a better example of an upbringing that hits on every risk factor and represents a complete failure in every dimension necessary for an emotionally healthy child than **Aileen Wuornos.** A textbook case in how to destroy a child. I have mentioned before that not all people raised in specific dysfunctional environments turn into criminals, not all people with specific cognitive traits become murderers, but the combination of factors Aileen experienced made her chances of a normal life so slim, it is in the realm of lottery odds. Aileen was the daughter of teenage parents; dad was 18, mom was 14 when they married. Mom had her first child at 15, and Aileen at 16, two months after her parents divorced. Dad was already in jail by the time she was born, she never met him prior to his suicide in jail when she was 13. Shortly before her fourth birthday her mother abandoned her with her maternal grandparents who legally adopted her. Being abandoned so early, Aileen was easily led to believe the grandparents were her biological parents. She was not told the truth until she was eleven. The grandparents, both alcoholic, were physically and sexually abusive. At age 14 she became pregnant by one of her grandfather's friends. The child was put up for adoption. Just months afterward her grandmother died of alcohol-related liver failure, and a few months after that her grandfather kicked her out of the house with no means of support.

Not many options in 1971 for a 15-year-old victim of physical and sexual abuse, with no family, no friends, no social support, and no means of financial support.

There is a frequent pattern seen both in Aileen Wuornos and previously in Richard Kuklinski when emerging from abusive environments. As a survival mechanism one might be passive in the abusive environment to avoid triggering the abuser but become abusive themselves outside the environment as a self-protective mechanism to avoid abuse by others. In both cases this manifested itself in short tempers and easily triggered aggressive behavior.

The emotional abuse Aileen experienced, much like Kuklinski, meant she was not going to see herself as someone capable of functioning in a regular workplace; her short temper and violent outbursts would make this even more difficult, not to mention, who would hire a homeless 15-year-old? Sex work was the direction the environment was pushing her, and one that likely paid better than minimum wage.

Why do victims of sexual abuse turn toward sex work? Doesn't it seem like a perpetuation of the abuse rather than an escape from it? There is no "one size fits all" answer to this; there is incredible variation, and it depends on the specific type of sex work and degree of interaction with the customer. I will focus specifically on the "street walker" category because this was the category Aileen was in. Motivation can range from surrender and self-destruction (Ulibarri, et al., 2013) to taking something which was once out of their control and taking control of it by making it a choice and perceiving it as power over the customer (Bell, 2009), with an entire spectrum of variation and risk in-between. A wild card is the risk posed by the customers. Is a given customer a shy person looking for a typical sexual experience, or a Gary Ridgway? Men who seek the "street walker" are more prone to show traits associated with sexual coercion (Farley, et al., 2017) and have a depersonalized and dehumanized view toward the sex worker. No surprise this would make them potentially more likely to seek aggressive sexual activity and be more dangerous to the worker.

As a side note, the internet has brought a change to sex-work with the opportunity to avoid direct contact with customers, and in some cases know little or nothing about customers other than that they are paying for access to the content. This has brought about the growth of a new demographic of sex worker, the person who is simply exploring their sexuality and in many cases feeling empowered by the income being generated without the same risk that would come from direct contact.

I hate to shatter anyone's rosy nostalgia for the 1970s and 1980s, but those were the worst decades since before WWII to be living on the street and exposed to crime. Almost every category of crime and social problems were peaking in those decades, before a gradual decline began in the mid-1990s.

This was the world Aileen Wuornos was thrust into at the age of 15. Between 1974 and 1987 Aileen accumulated a long rap sheet across multiple states: DUI, disorderly conduct, weapons charges, assault, disturbing the peace, armed robbery (for which she served a year from 1982 into 1983) forged checks, car theft, etc. In 1976, after hitchhiking to Florida, she met a wealthy 69-year-old man (Lewis Gratz Fell, President of the local yacht club) which led to a very brief marriage of only 9 weeks. Shortly after the wedding she was arrested for assault at a bar, later in an argument with Fell she hit him with his own cane, leading to a restraining order and a quick annulment. Her first murder did not happen until 1989, with a spree of seven killings over the span of 12 months.

Let's come back to the "there are a lot of people who …" argument. There are many living a crime lifestyle like this who never resort to murder. Reportedly, between the ages of 14 and 24 Aileen attempted suicide at least six times (Myers, Gooch & Meloy, 2005) and despite her long criminal record, she had no charges of attempted murder. This seems to put her more in the risk category of self-harm than murder. What changed?

Richard Charles Mallory, a 51-year-old electronics store owner in Clearwater, Florida, who liked to drink, party with strippers, enjoy the company of sex workers, and carried with him a previous conviction of attempted rape. In November 1989 he picked up Aileen for sex, took her to an abandoned area, and instead of simply sex, he beat and sodomized her. She shot him in the chest multiple times and fled in his vehicle, abandoning it several miles away.

Aileen often claimed her murders were all in self-defense, but she later admitted only this first one was self-defense, the others were motivated by robbery. Which puts her in the category of "Comfort" serial killer, killing for money.

Why the sudden turn toward homicide? Given her history it is not hard to see how after committing a murder and getting away with it, she would realize she could use the promise of sex to attract men, who would have cash on them to pay for the service, and simply kill them and take the money without the need to engage in sex. Even so, it was six months before the next murder, followed by one murder each month for the next five months. Her final murder, a 62-year-old trucker, security guard, and reserve police officer, occurred after police were already looking for her. She was arrested less than two months later after having been tracked via a handprint left in the car of one of her victims, and fingerprints from pawnshop receipts where she had sold some of her victim's belongings. She was charged with six of the seven murders (one of her victims, Peter Abraham Siems, was never found), and received the death penalty for each count.

Public hatred for Aileen was intense, especially in the communities where she found her victims, not just because of the murders, but because several victims were considered upstanding members of the community who friends and family claimed would never seek out a sex worker, therefore they assumed she was hunting victims.

Female serial killers in general shock people more than their male counterparts because of the socialized stereotype of women being passive nurturers, and the assumption that any "real" man would be able to defend himself from a woman. Again, reality does not always match socialized norms or stereotypes.

Aileen was the subject of numerous documentaries, books, and films, including the 2003 film "Monster" featuring Charlize Theron and Christina Ricci, released just over a year after Aileen's execution by lethal injection in October 2002. In her last recorded interview, less than 24 hours before her execution, Aileen angrily lashed out at mass media for the money it had made from her story during the years she had been sitting on death row.

In his 1930 book "Behaviorism" John Watson, the father of behaviorism, famously said *"Give me a dozen healthy infants, well-formed, and my own specified world to bring them up in and I'll guarantee to take any one at random and train him to become any type of specialist I might select — doctor, lawyer, artist, merchant-chief and, yes, even beggar-man and thief, regardless of his talents, penchants, tendencies, abilities, vocations, and race of his ancestors."*

Aileen Wuornos, from birth to death, was a prototypical example of what Watson was talking about, and of everyone I am covering in this chapter, the most obvious example. But as you might be noticing, few of the serial killers we are covering were "predestined" to become killers. They required either the presence of triggering risk factors, the absence of corrective guidance, or both. Our next subject is no different.

Jeffrey Dahmer is another example of uninterrupted progression toward psychopathy. But unlike Aileen Wuornos, Dahmer's roots were molded by neglect rather than abuse.

Dahmer killed 17 young men, one in 1978, the other 16 between 1987 and 1991. He was fascinated in studying body parts and preserving parts of the skeletons, especially skulls. In one of his confessions he talked about wanting to make a shrine to himself including a series of preserved skulls and two intact skeletons. To add to the public horror, he was also known to integrate body parts such as heart, liver, biceps, etc., into dinner recipes for consumption, and he attempted to create a passive zombie-like partner by drilling holes into the skulls of living victims and injecting acid or boiling water. His spree escalated dramatically after he moved into the Oxford apartments in Milwaukee Wisconsin, the first residence where he truly lived alone. During that relatively short time he claimed 12 victims in only 14 months before finally being arrested in the summer of 1991.

Dahmer was born in May 1960 in Milwaukee, Wisconsin. There are some contradictory stories about whether his mother was very doting or very neglectful. Given most stories about her she likely had an attention-craving personality disorder along with either hypochondriasis or somatization disorder (both involve believing you have an illness when one does not exist). Her frequent claims of being ill led to spending much time in bed, and Jeffrey was often left on his own. His father, initially a chemistry student and later chemist was frequently away from home, and when he was home there were frequent arguments with his wife. Dahmer reported never feeling a sense of family solidity, and most certainly never had a firm attachment to either parent (Norris, 1992).

His fascination with dead animals began when he was four years old, watching his father remove animal bones from under their home. Dahmer began collecting animal bones wherever he could find them, including dissecting roadkill to examine organs and extract bones. His father, considering his son to be displaying a budding scientific interest, taught him how to clean and preserve bones. Parallel to this time period was his mother's increasing use of anti-anxiety medications (at least once using them in a suicide attempt) and sleeping pills. This likely influenced Dahmer to later use sleeping pills mixed into drinks to sedate his victims.

Here is where we get to the first critical period. Dahmer's interest in the internal organs and skeletons of animals was left unchecked and unguided by his parents (one of his elementary school teachers even felt he displayed signs of abandonment). What if Dahmer had a parent who took a greater interest in what seemed a growing interest and hobby for Jeffrey? Not just directing it more toward the scientific (or even artistic if he showed any interest in taxidermy), but also putting boundaries on it.

Earlier I asked, at what point of either size or complexity is a living thing perceived to have value? Separately, regardless of size and complexity, cultures will define which animals are pets and which are food. Culture will encourage perceiving food animals as objects of value rather than living things of value. And the top of the value chain are pets.

Jeffrey Dahmer had no pets growing up. His initiation into animals was from the inside out: Bones and organs. He never had guidance or socialization which would put animals on any hierarchy of value, they all went into a single category. How would that translate into perception of strangers and the value of their lives?

Dahmer did not start out as the person he later became. He started taking gradual baby steps in that direction which were never challenged or corrected. He was allowed to spiral slowly into what he later became.

By the time he was 14 he had started drinking, often in the morning, sneaking it into school, and sometimes appearing drunk in class. This was the beginning of a problem that would follow him through adulthood until his eventual arrest and was likely a big contributing factor in allowing impulsive urges to become physical acts. Remember from earlier chapters, the frontal lobes are impulse control, decision making, and perception of consequence. Anything which disrupts the frontal lobes disrupts those functions, and alcohol, as a depressant, slows the functioning of the frontal lobes.

At puberty, Dahmer realized he was homosexual (Masters, 1993), but did not tell anyone. As is typical at puberty he also began to have sexual fantasies. A person with Dahmer's upbringing, one of instability and the absence of any sense of control over the environment will compensate by having fantasies of control, such as Gary Ridgway's fantasies of harming his mother. At puberty the addition of sexual fantasy can combine with control fantasies creating what Dahmer experienced: Powerful fantasies of completely controlling male sexual partners. At 16 his fantasies directed outward at a male jogger he saw frequently who he found attractive. Fantasies around this person escalated to the point that Dahmer hid in bushes with a baseball bat, with the plan of knocking the man unconscious and using him sexually. He never carried it out, but this was an obvious sign the fantasies were becoming motivations for behavior. A blow to the head with a bat could have easily killed the jogger, but at this point Dahmer's motivation was not murder; it was to have a passive, unconscious victim.

During his senior year in high school his parents separated. Dad moved out, and just before graduation Dahmer's mother and younger brother left to live with other relatives, leaving Dahmer alone in the family home. This final removal of any sort of moderating influence opened the door for extreme fantasy to become extreme behavior. A mere three weeks after graduating from high school, Dahmer picked up a male hitchhiker and lured him back to the house with the promise of beer. When the hitchhiker started talking about women, confirming he was heterosexual, Dahmer knew his advances would be rejected. When the hitchhiker tried to leave the home, Dahmer struck him from behind with a dumbbell, then strangled him to death. He now had the ultimate in a passive and controlled sexual partner. He later destroyed the remains by dissolving the flesh in solution and crushing the bones.

Let's pause here for a moment. First, we need to always be cautious when killers are giving accounts of early behavior, including claims of their drives and motivations at the time. In general people tend to skew interpretation of behaviors in their distant past to align better with their current behaviors and attitudes. Dahmer's victim sustained serious injury from the blows to the head, but ultimately died by strangulation. At this point in time, Dahmer was more interested in an unconscious victim than a dead victim. He was primarily a serial rapist. Strangling the hitchhiker might have been part of his sex play, and the death an accident. Dahmer dissected parts of the body afterward, then buried the remains in his back yard. He later dug up the remains, dissolved the organs and crushed the bones. This would indicate the death and disposal were not preplanned, and fear of being caught made him hurriedly bury the body and later realized he needed to do a better job of disposal.

What support is there for the claim he did not intend murder? Because it was nine years before he did it again.

Six weeks after the killing, his father returned to the home to find Dahmer living there alone. At his father's urging he enrolled in college, only lasting one year, then joined the Army, which stretched into two years, both ventures ended because of Dahmer's excessive drinking. By December 1981, when Dahmer was 21 years old, he was sent to live with his grandmother in the hope that her influence could help him stop drinking and find a secure job. Her presence stifled his predatory behavior but did not stop the drinking or immediately help him keep a job. In 1985 he finally found stable employment working the night shift at the Milwaukee Ambrosia Chocolate Factory. This would end up being his longest stretch of continuous employment.

It is impossible to know if these dormant years were the product of self-control driven by anxiety over the first murder and a desire to never do that again, or if it was simply the environment not providing a trigger. It was likely both. At one point Dahmer stole a male mannequin from a store and used it as a sexual prop. He disposed of it when his grandmother found it. He read about the funeral of a young man and attempted to dig up the body to use it sexually. He failed because, as he remembers, it was too difficult trying to dig it up.

An environmental trigger came in 1985 when, reading alone at a library, he was sexually propositioned by a man. Dahmer did not respond, but it stirred his interest and motivated him to start seeking out gay clubs and bathhouses in Milwaukee. It was then he started hooking up and having sexual encounters. He found these encounters frustrating because the partners had their own needs and desires, while Dahmer wanted a completely passive partner who would not resist anything he wanted to do. As a solution he started drugging his partners to sleep and sexually assaulting them. By his own account, he saw his sexual targets as nothing more than objects for pleasure.

It was not until November 1987 that Dahmer committed his second murder. He later claimed to have no plan to kill the person, nor did he have any memory of the murder. He lured a victim to a hotel, drugged him with the intent of using him for sex, and woke the next morning to find the man in bed next to him beaten to death. He purchased a large suitcase to get the body out of the hotel, took it to his grandmother's basement where, over the span of a couple weeks, he dismembered the corpse and disposed of it in the garbage. He cleaned and briefly retained the skull for sexual pleasure before also disposing of it. Cleaning and retaining skulls would become a consistent part of Dahmer's pattern.

Whether murder had been intended or not, this was the trigger that started Dahmer actively hunting victims with the intent of killing them. His next victim was less than two months later, a 14-year-old male sex worker, and another victim a month later. Both disposed of by dismembering, both skulls retained for a time as sex toys. Another attempt one month later was interrupted by his grandmother, who heard Dahmer in the basement with another man. Dahmer drugged the man, but decided it was too risky to kill him. This near discovery seemed to scare him away from murder for a time.

Six months later his grandmother kicked him out. With the final removal of any environmental constraints on his impulses, the floodgates were about to open. Just two days after moving into an apartment, he drugged and molested a 13-year-old boy he had lured to his apartment. The boy escaped and Dahmer was arrested. Dahmer's father hired Attorney Gerald Boyle to defend Dahmer. Boyle would defend him again three years later. Dahmer was given several psychological screenings to be presented in his defense, among the results was a diagnosis of Schizoid Personality Disorder.

There were many different diagnoses of Dahmer suggested in the days and years after his arrest, some of them, such as Borderline Personality Disorder, likely influenced by the behavior demonstrated by his mother. Some diagnosed him posthumously with Autism Spectrum Disorder, (Silva, Ferrari, & Leong, 2002) while others warn of the dangers of doing so (Palermo & Bogaerts, 2015). It is always risky to apply diagnosis based on archived data without firsthand examination of the individual.

Of all of these diagnoses, the initial diagnosis of Schizoid Personality Disorder was the best fit and the most accurate diagnosis, granted, we cannot say that if today's diagnostic criteria for Autism Spectrum had existed when Dahmer was examined, he might have received that diagnosis instead. This is understandable because the two share many features.

The primary diagnostic criteria for Schizoid Personality Disorder is "A pervasive pattern of detachment from social relationships and a restricted range of expression of emotions in interpersonal settings, beginning by early adulthood and present in a variety of contexts" (American Psychiatric Association, 2013) requiring at least four of the following seven: Neither desires nor enjoys chose relationships, almost always chooses solitary activities, has little, if any, interest in sexual experiences with another person, takes pleasure in few, if any, activities, lacks close friends or confidants other than first-degree relatives, appears indifferent to the praise or criticism of others, and shows emotional coldness, detachment, or flattened affectivity.

The one of those seven which obviously does not fit Dahmer is interest in sexual activities, but he never wanted a mutual sexual experience, he wanted another person as a passive object with no emotional attachment. Give Dahmer access to a realistic sex doll and it might have sufficiently satisfied his cravings that he would not have sought out human partners.

Between Dahmer's arrest and his sentencing, he claimed another victim. He insisted he was not actively looking for a victim, but while at a gay bar the man struck up a conversation which led to a hook-up.

For his original arrest, Dahmer was sentenced to five years' probation, and one year in corrections, with work release so he could keep his job. He was paroled two months early. In May 1990 he moved into his final, infamous apartment at 924 North 25th Street (infamous to the point the building was later demolished). It was here he would kill 12 people in the span of 14 months and adopt the behaviors for which he is most remembered, including keeping body parts, eating some internal organs, and creating a "shrine" of skeletal remains.

Five of his last victims could have been saved if not for the reckless disregard of two police officers. In May 1991, Dahmer lured 14-year-old Konerak Sinthasomphone to his apartment where he drugged him, sexually assaulted him, and drilled a small hole into his head to inject acid (trying to create a passive "living zombie" for his pleasure). The boy escaped, running naked into the neighborhood where two women found him and called police. When police arrived, Dahmer came out, calmly talked to the officers, telling them the boy was his 19-year-old boyfriend who had been drinking too much and fled the apartment after an argument. The officers did not pursue the issue further, and even escorted Dahmer and the boy back to Dahmer's apartment.

Why were the officers so quick to release him? Let's look at the cultural environment in the U.S. during this time. Whatever advances the gay community had made in the 1960s and 1970s was destroyed by the AIDS epidemic in the 1980s. The homosexual community was once again seen as deviant, and by some, who did not understand how AIDS was transmitted, a danger to public safety. Once the officers heard the boy was in a "gay" relationship, their stereotypes of gay lifestyle no longer perceived the scene as suspicious. It is completely possible that if Dahmer had not labeled the boy as his gay lover, the police might have been more suspicious and investigated further.

Dahmer killed the boy that evening and went on to kill four more people over the following two months before his final intended victim managed to escape and police finally investigated Dahmer's apartment.

Dahmer was indicted on 15 counts of murder and given multiple life sentences. In November 1994 he was beaten to death in a prison bathroom.

Dahmer obviously fits the category of "organized" serial killer due to intentionally and calmly hunting victims and carefully disposing of bodies. His motivations were both "lust" and "power/control."

Tommy Lynn Sells was convicted and sentenced to death for only one murder but is suspected in more than 20 killings from 1980 to 1999.

Sells is well within the category of disorganized killer. His murders were impulsive, spontaneous, and opportunistic. Other than killing potential witnesses he made little effort to cover his tracks. Living a transient lifestyle meant he did not stay in one place long enough to be identified or caught. His motivations contain an element of power/control, but he is mostly in the thrill subset of the hedonistic category. He described watching someone die as producing a rush like taking a drug (ABC News, 2010). If we were to apply the psychopath or sociopath labels to him, he would be a classic sociopath.

Like the others we have covered, there are definite childhood roots to his later behavior, both environmental and developmental. Sells was a fraternal twin born in 1964, to a single mother with three children from a previous relationship. When they were 18 months old, both twins developed spinal meningitis; the other twin died as a result, and a short time later Sells was sent to live with an aunt. Two years later, when the aunt wanted to adopt Sells, his mother took him back.

There is little information about why the mother sent him away while keeping the other children, but there are some clues we can extract from his illness and his later behavior.

Meningitis can cause short term cognitive and behavioral effects. In some people the effects can be long term (Viner et al., 2012), including aggression, problems with memory, and problems with executive function (the frontal lobes; impulse control and decision making). In short, when occurring in young children it can cause developmental issues which were not previously present. It was likely overwhelming for a single mother with three other children suddenly handling a child who needed extra care; it would make sense sending him to a relative willing to help. This is the first point in development where a single choice likely set his path in the wrong direction. Instead of allowing the aunt to adopt him, his mother took him back.

There are many indicators of neglect by the mother: Sells reportedly began stealing alcohol from his mother when he was 7-years old. When he was eight, he was molested repeatedly by a neighbor. These things alone would have caused behavioral and emotional issues, but when he was 13 his mother finally gave up. She took her other kids and moved away, leaving him alone in the house. By 14 he was homeless, living the life of a drifter. According to Sells, he committed his first murder when he was 15, killing a homeowner during a burglary.

He is sometimes called the "Cross Country Killer" because he traveled so often and covered so many states. His murders were sometimes driven by sexual assault, but more often rage. He killed several single mothers and their children, and in one notorious instance a husband and pregnant wife. The assault caused spontaneous labor, so Sells killed the baby as well. He would travel with other hitchhikers for a time and either become angry at them or bored with them and kill them. Ultimately, one of his victims, a 10-year-old girl, survived her throat being slashed after witnessing Sells murder her friend, and was able to identify him. He was quickly arrested.

It is unknown how many people Sells killed during his life. Some of his confessions were thought to have been false, an effort to work the system by appearing valuable to law enforcement in solving old cases. They flew him around the country and took him to many locations where he claimed he had dumped bodies. He might have thought being valuable to the police in that way might save him from the death penalty, or it was merely an easy way to get out and travel rather than sit in a jail cell, but once he was convicted and sentenced to death in Texas the state would not allow him to be extradited for other cases. One of his confessions was of killing a 10-year-old boy in Illinois in 1997. He also tried to kill the mother, but she fought him off. The mother, Julie Rea Harper, was arrested for the crime and convicted on only circumstantial evidence. Sells' confession was detailed enough that Harper was granted another trial, and despite the prosecution insisting Sells' confession was false, Harper was found not guilty and released.

Tommy Lynn Sells was executed on April 3, 2014, in Texas. Over 20 cases have been linked to him, but according to his confessions he likely killed close to 100 people over the span of 20 years.

Let's wrap this up with the big dog: **Ted Bundy.** The prototype of the categories: Psychopath, Organized, and Power/Control, with a heavy element of the Lust subset of Hedonistic, especially in his earlier killings. Cannot write a book like this without including Bundy, despite it being more difficult to put him into the "progression toward killing" template I have applied to the others.

What makes Bundy difficult are the different accounts he gave different interviewers and biographers (Kendall, 1981; Michaud, 2000; Rule, 1980). He especially muddied the water after his conviction and death sentences, likely in order to delay his execution indefinitely by making himself appear valuable to detectives investigating unsolved cases. Authorities believe Bundy was researching unsolved cases to determine which cases might have matched his timeline, and in many cases confessed to killings without identifying victim or location to bargain his way into another delay of execution. He likely tweaked his personal history with each interviewer based on what would appeal to the interviewer. For example, Bundy's final interview was with Dr. James Dobson, leader of the evangelical group "Focus on the Family" and an outspoken critic of pornography. It was during this interview that Bundy claimed to have been raised in a good Christian household but was corrupted by the pornography he would find in dumpsters around town. That final interview is also a classic example of how a predator can appear sincere. I use the interview in class (it is easy to find online by searching "Bundy final interview") so the class can experience the feeling of Bundy seemingly being honest and trying to be helpful in identifying the roots of violent behavior. If you watch the video, note how calm he appears despite being less than 24 hours from his execution. Compare that with the final interview of Aileen Wuornos 24 hours before her execution.

His early history is mostly consistent across various biographers: Bundy was born in Vermont in 1946 in a "Home for Unwed Mothers." There are several suggestions of his biological father, but none were absolutely confirmed. He initially lived with his maternal grandparents but was raised to believe they were his biological parents and his mother was his older sister. This led some to suspect he might have been the product of incest between his mother and grandfather, but DNA tests years later eliminated this possibility. There are various accounts of how Bundy learned of his parentage, but most agree it was not until his early 20s that he learned the truth.

The only evidence of abnormal behavior in early childhood is an often-repeated account by his aunt who says she woke one night to find kitchen knives on her bed and 3-year-old Bundy standing next to the bed smiling. However, there should be more accounts than this if he was displaying antisocial behavior at such a young age.

His grandmother was prone to severe depression sometimes requiring electroconvulsive therapy treatments (electroshock), and by neighbor's accounts the grandfather was an alcoholic prone to physical violence and abuse to animals. It is hard to determine how much this might have shaped early development because Bundy and his mother moved to Tacoma, Washington when he was 4 years old.

There is something we need to ask at this point: How did 4-year-old Ted perceive his "sister" taking him away from their "parents" and his other supposed siblings and moving to a new city so far away? There is almost no way this could not have created resentment. This seems to be supported by Bundy's refusal to accept his new adopted father, Johnny Bundy, when he entered the family a year later. A child of four might not wonder why his sister's new husband would adopt him and treat him like a son, but he would definitely feel like an outsider in this environment, especially as his "sister" started having children with the new father figure and focused more attention on them.

Bundy claimed to have felt isolated as a teen-ager, with little or no understanding of how interpersonal relationships worked but was remembered by classmates as being well known and well liked (Rule, 1980). These two accounts are not contradictory because one comes from Bundy's self-perception, while the other comes from outside observation. It is frequent that people who interact with us will perceive us much differently from how we perceive ourselves.

There were many psychiatric evaluations performed on Bundy after his final arrest and conviction; they read like a dinner buffet of diagnoses, including Bipolar Disorder, Antisocial Personality Disorder (doesn't take a clinician to suggest that one) and because it was the 1980's, Multiple Personality Disorder. Let's talk about that one for a moment because Bundy's difficulty connecting with people, and his later claims that he had sudden "dark" shifts in personality, fit in to this. Not Multiple Personality itself, but what is today seen as conditions which led to the belief in Multiple Personality.

Multiple Personality Disorder has always been widely seen within the field of psychology as a fake disorder. So why did it make it into the third edition of the Diagnostic and Statistical Manual of Mental Disorders in 1980? Because there was an explosion of reported cases in the 1970s and 1980s, causing the disorder to be slipped in, not based on any empirical evidence, but on the number of influential clinicians making a lot of money with the diagnosis, and the public interest in the condition.

Prior to the early 1970s, Multiple Personality Disorder was so rare it was thought by some professionals to be a myth, or at best an exaggerated manifestation of an attention-seeking disorder combined with psychosis. Fewer than 100 cases had ever been documented.

What happened? The publication of the book "Sybil" in 1973 (Schreiber, 1973) and the release in 1976 of the film adaptation featuring Sally Field. This produced an explosion of reported cases, almost all in the United States. But there was something else which created suspicion in clinical professionals right away. Sybil was the first case of its kind. The first to feature more than three unique personalities, and the first to be solidly connected to an abusive upbringing. The problem with the surge of cases is that none of them resembled traditional Multiple Personality cases, they all resembled Sybil's case. Patients displayed the symptoms from the book and movie, therefore data from case studies represented the book and movie, which led to the diagnostic criteria in 1980 coming from what turned out to be a fictionalized source. Sybil did not have Multiple Personality Disorder (Rieber, 2006), the case of Sybil was created by her psychiatrist who had already signed a contract for a book about Multiple Personality Disorder.

Many people think the renamed "Dissociative Identify Disorder" (American Psychiatric Association, 2013) is Multiple Personality Disorder, but it is merely a subset of the cases which previously were thought to be MPD.

If Multiple Personality was never a real thing, then what was going on with people who seemed to experience it? And where would Bundy fall within it? Some were faking the disorder for personal gain, such as attention-seeking or to get out of trouble. For example, Kenneth Bianchi, one of the "Hillside Stranglers" attempted to claim Multiple Personality as a defense; saying he had no memory of the murders and they were all performed by his other personalities. Some people had personality disorders which included psychotic episodes when under stress. Many had very common conditions but were misdiagnosed by clinicians who had personal financial interest in diagnosing MPD (the "treatments" could go on for years and involved counseling each personality individually), but in the case of people who did seem to have obvious sudden shifts in personality the most likely culprit was Temporal Lobe Epilepsy, in which some people will experience changes in mood, impairment in impulse control and decision making, and anterograde amnesia for hours after experiencing an episode (Waxman & Geschwind, 1975; Hermann, et al., 2000; Alley, et al., 2014). Temporal Lobe seizures exist on a spectrum from severe (which are obvious to observers and often harmful to the individual) to more mild (a brief "blanking out" sometimes called "absence seizure" which are not obvious to observers and not encoded by the individual). Reports of Bundy suddenly turning "dark" and experiencing a rapid change in temperament or behavior could be such a sign.

Bipolar Disorder could also fit the cycles of Bundy's behavior and his sense that when the urge came, he had little or no control over it. It would also explain some of the reckless behavior and overconfidence which got him caught twice.

By official accounts, Bundy's attacks began in January 1974 (he claimed he started before then, and some investigators believe he could have started killing in his teens despite never offering specific details that could connect him to any unsolved murders). His first two attacks were break-ins, attacking his victims as they slept. Both University of Washington students, both living in basement apartments. The first, severely beaten and sexually assaulted, survived the attack. The second was a month later, also a break-in, but the victim was taken to Bundy's dump site on Taylor mountain (off Highway 18 east of Seattle) where the body was dismembered. He then started actively abducting people in public. He initially displayed a cycle, killing one person each month, until June 1974, when he killed two people within a week of each other, then a month later killed two people on the same day, both abducted from the same place (Lake Sammamish State Park). This last one was his most blatant, being done in broad daylight. It also produced the first witness sketch, the name "Ted" and a description of his car.

Some speculate, because the first victim survived, that Bundy's intent was sexual assault, not murder, and fear of getting caught caused him to take that final step, but a later account by the victim suggests Bundy was scared off by a roommate in another room who talked in their sleep (Kappel & Lasola, 2020).

Between the two victims in June, Bundy changed his dump site from Taylor Mountain to a location near Issaquah, Washington, a few minutes up Interstate 90 going west from his previous dump site. It is unknown why he changed sites, but his two victims in July were also dumped at that site.

He also displayed an early pattern of hunting college students and traveling the northwest to avoid hitting any place twice. After his attack on two University of Washington students, his attack in March was two hours south at the Evergreen State College near Olympia, a month later he crossed the mountains east and abducted a student from Central Washington State College (now Central Washington University) in Ellensburg. And in May he travelled down to Oregon State University, in Corvallis, south of Portland. Despite his travels, he brought all these victims back to the Seattle area and dumped them at

Taylor Mountain.

Up to that point he was exhibiting a pattern which represented preplanning to avoid being caught. But his killings in June and July of 1974 were a reckless change in that pattern. He seemed to be more spontaneous, grabbing one victim from near a bar, another from an alley, and finally the two in broad daylight from Lake Sammamish State Park.

He then went silent for three months. What triggered the start of the murders and possibly influenced the pause?

Let's roll back a couple years and look at Bundy's history of romantic relationships. He was in and out of several relationships during his University years, but three became on-again/off-again long term. The first was Stephanie Brooks, who he met while both were students at the University of Washington and started dating in 1967. The relationship lasted a year before Brooks ended it, saying Bundy was immature and lacked motivation. Most of Bundy's biographers feel this is a keystone moment. Bundy was devasted by the breakup and briefly traveled east, enrolling for one semester at Temple University. It is during this time Bundy later claimed he killed two people in Atlantic City, but to other investigators he made contradictory claims. It is also thought it was during this year he checked his birth records and discovered his true parentage.

Think about the impact of the break-up and the discovery of his true parentage happening so close. Roll back to young Bundy, thinking his sister had taken him from his parents and moved across the country to a place where he did not know anyone; where the only source of emotional support and familiarity was his sister. She very quickly became emotionally attached to someone else, perceived by young Bundy as rejection, then began having more children, further rejection and a sense of "being replaced." There is no sense of reciprocated attachment, but a strong sense of being marginalized, and a feeling of being alone. Young Bundy had no sense of control over anything happening to him, which would lead to an insatiable desire for control in adulthood. By itself these are traits commonly found in adults who come from neglectful and unstable early environments. He had strong feelings for Stephanie Brooks, which were not reciprocated, and then she not only broke up with him, she moved from Seattle back to her family home in California.

Did his later victim preference as far as hair color, style, and length, as well as age, physical characteristics and education come from this painful break-up? Maybe. Many biographers feel it did. But it could also be that the physical characteristics were simply his preference, so he would be attracted to them both as relationships and victims. As for being educated; Bundy's environment was a University campus, so that was going to be a trait shared by everyone he encountered.

By autumn 1969 he was back in Seattle and quickly fell into a stormy relationship with Elizabeth Kloepfer, a single mom who would be an on-again/off-again relationship well after his eventual arrest and incarceration. While dating Bundy, she would be one of the first people to alert detectives that he could be the killer they were looking for.

By mid-1970 Bundy was enrolled again at the University of Washington, this time majoring in Psychology, and this time performing at a much higher level than before. He graduated in 1972, was accepted into law school in 1973, and during the summer, while on a trip to California, reconnected with Stephanie Brooks, who was impressed by how he had pulled himself together. For several months he balanced relationships with both Brooks and Kloepfer, without either knowing about the other. Brooks would fly up to spend time with Bundy.

And here we reach the truly critical point. Bundy suddenly broke off the relationship with Brooks at the same time he began his first string of attacks. During this string he began dating his third "on-again/off-again" partner: Carol Ann Boone, who would eventually testify on his behalf, and supply possibly one of the more bizarre endings to his story.

After seven months of stalking victims, two factors likely led to the brief pause in the killing. The first is that the daylight abductions at Lake Sammamish State Park led to local media revealing his first name, a sketch of his face, and a description of his car. The second is that in August, around the time his pattern would predict another victim, he received a second law school acceptance, this time to the University of Utah. He accepted, and moved to Salt Lake City, leaving Kloepfer behind in Seattle.

This is a point, much like Dahmer, where the police let a big opportunity slip. When the descriptions were broadcast on local media, Kloepfer, as well as one of Bundy's co-workers and one of his professors, recognized the face and the car and obviously the name Ted. But police did not think such a clean-cut man going to law school was likely to be the person they were looking for. Which raises the question, what "kind of person" did they think they were looking for? Three different people had pointed them toward a suspect who fit the description of the face, the name, and the car.

By this time Bundy was likely feeling invincible, and his urges were becoming more frequent. A contributor to this? He made it out of Seattle without being caught, even after his name, his car, and a sketch of his face had been released to media. The person driven by a need for power and control was feeling powerful and in control. He controlled his victims, and he controlled the system trying to catch him. If there had been any caution to avoid being caught, the cautions were receding, which also meant he was likely to become more reckless.

Becoming less cautious the longer you go without experiencing consequence is a common human trait. We will engage in risky behavior (such as driving in winter weather conditions) knowing we need to be cautious, but as we go longer without a bad outcome, we become less cautious. Rather than consciously understanding that our caution is the reason there has not been a bad outcome, we become overconfident, increasing the chance of a bad outcome. In general, if you get away with something, you are more likely to do it again. Just as Dahmer's killings increased once he was living alone with no environmental constraints (such as the presence of his grandmother), Bundy's drive to kill felt less restrained by not being caught, and by moving out of the area. He had a clean slate.

He did not wait until reaching Utah before killing again; he killed a hitchhiker in Idaho on the way. He killed at least three people in communities in Utah in October 1974 (his most prolific verified single-month total), and when an intended victim escaped his car in November, he drove to another community and grabbed another victim just hours later.

He did display an ability to restrain his behavior. He had a new hunting ground in the Utah and Colorado areas, so when he would return to the Seattle area for visits, he did not take any further victims. In Utah, his monthly cycle continued with some pauses when Kloepfer, Boone, and other acquaintances from the Seattle area would stop by to visit him. Of his six victims between January and June 1975, only one was ever found.

Kloepfer continued to contact authorities in both Seattle and Salt Lake City but also continued her relationship with Bundy, which might raise a question. If he was overcome by homicidal impulses, why did he never kill the people he dated or lived with? For the same reason Gary Ridgway did not kill his wives; he would be an immediate suspect. More than likely any relationship frustration was vented on strangers who could not be directly tied to him.

In August 1975 he was pulled over in Utah when an officer saw him driving slowly through a neighborhood in the early morning hours and sped away when he saw the officer. Incriminating evidence was found in the car, but not enough to keep him detained. This formally put him on the radar and authorities in both Seattle and Salt Lake City started watching him. He was charged with kidnapping in the case of the victim who had escaped in November 1974 but there was not enough evidence to charge him with any murders. And this is where his case becomes legendary in True Crime circles. He was caught planning several escapes from jail, escaped once and was on the run for a week before being caught (he was pulled over for driving erratically, not because he was recognized as a fugitive), and on December 30, 1977 managed a final escape from his cell in Colorado. Little more than a week later he was in Florida.

He was in the clear, with a physical appearance that was so common it did not take much of a disguise for him to hide in plain sight; he could have easily remained free and never been caught. On the surface you would expect someone as organized as Bundy to personally revel in having beaten the system and the people who tried to convict him. But Bundy was also driven by the power/control need, and when needs such as these are a key component of the survival instinct, it is impossible to satisfy them no matter how much true control exists in the environment. This is generally true any time childhood abuse or neglect has attached a need to a survival instinct, such as need for attention or need for a caretaker figure. Even when the environment supplies these needs, the individual continues to seek them and never feels completely satisfied.

Barely a week after arriving in Florida, Bundy went on his most prolific, most violent, and final spree, attacking four students in a Florida State University sorority house, and another in an apartment eight blocks away. Three of the five survived, but all suffered severe injuries. He fled, a month later abducting a Junior High School student from her school (during school hours) before finally being pulled over due to driving a stolen car.

Not only was it odd that the killing continued so soon after escaping, when he had given himself a great opportunity disappear and never get caught, but this spree was different in the number of victims at one time, and the number who survived. These attacks reflect a profile more often seen in an unorganized sociopathic killer than in a controlled and organized killer. It was estimated his attack in the sorority house took less than fifteen minutes, and the attack in the apartment eight blocks away was also short and left a surviving victim. It was not until his final victim, three weeks later, that he once again displayed his typical profile.

Did something unusual happen in that one event? Or did Bundy have a second killing style that was never previously associated with him? That would open the door for many other unsolved murders to possibly be due to Bundy and raise more questions about his psychological profile.

Would any of the root causes we've covered explain how Bundy could potentially possess both killing styles at different times? This is purely speculative, but yes. Bipolar Disorder could explain his typical cycles (although it would need to be the Rapid Cycling type), and the immediate aftereffects of Temporal Lobe Epilepsy could explain how his homicidal drive could vent in a more disorganized way. The problem with this speculation is that Bundy should be more likely to experience amnesia for the episodes following a Temporal Lobe incident, but he seemed to have perfect memory of the Sorority attack. It is not impossible that Bundy had another side, but most of the evidence does not support it.

So, what triggered the violent Sorority house attack? We can never know for sure. It could have been an encounter with one or more of the students; perhaps Bundy propositioned a student looking for a date and was rebuffed in a way that angered him, or maybe he intended a more typical deadly attack and was spooked. One of the survivors believes that headlights shining through a window might have scared him off.

His trial was predictably a circus. His need for control led him to serve as his own attorney, create a mockery of the proceedings, and in a final bizarre twist, Carol Ann Boone, one of his juggled relationships while also seeing Kloepfer, moved to Florida to be near him during his trials, testified in his defense, and legally married him during one of the sentencing hearings. She became pregnant and gave birth to a daughter; Bundy's only known child. She divorced him in 1986 after finally realizing, as he confessed to more murders and gave more graphic detail, that he was not innocent. Boone and her daughter returned to the Northwest. Their whereabouts today are unknown. It has been said they are living under assumed names to avoid any connection to Bundy.

It was after the convictions and during the long process leading toward eventual execution that Bundy gave multiple interviews and offered dozens of confessions, often changing stories or details of stories from one interview to the next. Some of the details he supplied did fit with forensic details of the cases, others did not, so it is important to apply caution when assuming that anything Bundy said from within prison was accurate and not simply an attempt to play the system or delay execution. In 1984 he offered his expertise as a serial killer to help investigators solve open cases (it was then he met with detectives investigating the Green River killer, Gary Ridgway) to make himself valuable as a long-term asset to be spared execution. His original execution date was March 4, 1986, but through numerous stays and appeals it was not carried out until January 24, 1989.

There is much myth and rumor around Ted Bundy's brain, with

many sources claiming his brain was removed and studied, with no abnormalities being found. There is no evidence his brain was removed. What did happen was an intensive physical and psychological examination which included x-rays of his brain. Some researchers believe these x-rays show a small cyst in one temporal lobe and lesions in the frontal lobes indicative of damage which can occur from abuse. There is much speculation that this is the reason he was a killer. We always have to be cautious about global assessments like this about brain structure and behavior because we miss one inescapable point: Ted Bundy was functional the majority of the time, performing well when he focused on studies, graduating from the University of Washington, working on political campaigns, having relationships with people (without killing them), and interacting normally with people in a way that caused disbelief when they discovered his crimes. Behavioral and psychological components can vary by environment, but it is harder for structural damage to only emerge in specific situations. The other consideration is, how common are these structural differences in the general population? We can say structural anomalies plus psychological factors can increase the risk, but we still have the problem of 99.99% of Bundy's time being functional. It would have been much more useful to have had access to Functional Magnetic Resonance Imaging (fMRI) back then to see structure as well as how different areas of the brain functioned and communicated because those can fluctuate by mood and under stress.

Are there points where Ted Bundy's progression into a serial killer could have been interrupted? It is easy, and to a degree comforting, to hold to the belief that people like Bundy are born, not made, and not everyone who experiences the life Bundy experienced turns into a killer. But in every killer, there are a collection of individual components that come together to turn them into something dangerous and interrupting enough of those components can change the outcome.

There is a final point in dismissing the idea of killers simply being "born bad." If that were the case, that something genetic was at work producing these killers, then their numbers should stay consistent across time and demographics. But in the United States the 1970s through the 1990s were the Age of the Serial Killer. Since then the numbers have been steadily declining (Aamodt, 2016). Like almost all other crime statistics which began to decline in the mid-1990s, so did the incidence of serial killers.

I'll leave you with this to chew on and debate: The greatest number of serial killers in the United States were born between 1945 and 1965, as were the people most responsible for the peak years of murder overall in the U.S., the 1970s through the mid-1990s. The generations who followed them have produced lower rates of crime in almost every category.

Obviously, there were many famous serial killers I did not cover in this chapter: Dennis Rader, John Wayne Gacy, the Zodiac among others. I tried to grab a representative example from several broad categories, to cover them all would require its own book. Maybe that is a project for another day.

I hope I was successful in helping you get into the heads of some of these killers, understand where they come from, and understand how otherwise "normal" people could progress to abnormal extremes. How each of us can encounter the right series of events converging at the right time to create the risk of making a tragic impulsive choice. Or how we can see this progression in others and intervene before it is too late.

References

Aamodt, M. G. (2016, September 4). Serial killer statistics. Retrieved (insert date of retrieval) from http://maamodt.asp.radford.edu/serial killer information center/project description.htm

ABC News, (August 26, 2010), Nightline, "Tommy Lynn Sells - The Mind of a Psychopath."

ABC News, (January 6, 2006), "Yates Friend: I Begged Russell to Get Help" https://abcnews.go.com/GMA/story?id=126247&page=1

Abdalla-Filho, E., & Völlm, B. (2020). Does every psychopath have an antisocial personality disorder? *Revista brasileira de psiquiatria (Sao Paulo, Brazil: 1999), 42*(3), 241–242. https://doi.org/10.1590/1516-4446-2019-0762

Allely C, Minnis H, Thompson L, Wilson P, Gillberg C, "Neurodevelopmental and psychosocial risk factors in serial killers and mass murderers," Aggression and Violent Behavior, Volume 19, Issue 3, 2014, Pages 288-301, ISSN 1359-1789, https://doi.org/10.1016/j.avb.2014.04.004.

American Psychiatric Association. (2013). DIAGNOSTIC AND STATISTICAL MANUAL OF MENTAL DISORDERS (5th ed.). https://doi.org/10.1176/appi.books.9780890425596

APNEWS "Motorcyclist commits suicide after killing girl" Author: Henry Cutter, May 23, 1995. Retrieved from: https://apnews.com/article/82a608240f93d3be6220a063579fcde9

Ariely, D., & Loewenstein, G. (2006). The Heat of the Moment: The Effect of Sexual Arousal on Sexual Decision Making. Journal of Behavioral Decision Making, 19, 87-98. http://dx.doi.org/10.1002/bdm.501

Arnedo J, Svrakic DM, Del Val C, Romero-Zaliz R, Hernández-Cuervo H; Molecular Genetics of Schizophrenia Consortium, Fanous AH, Pato MT, Pato CN, de Erausquin GA, Cloninger CR, Zwir I. "Uncovering the hidden risk architecture of the schizophrenias: confirmation in three independent genome-wide association studies." Am J Psychiatry. 2015 Feb 1;172(2):139-53. doi: 10.1176/appi.ajp.2014.14040435. Epub 2014 Oct 31. Erratum in: Am J Psychiatry. 2014 Oct;171(10):1124. PMID: 25219520.

Asperger, H. (1944). Die "Autistischen Psychopathen" im Kindesalter. Archiv für Psychiatrie und Nervenkrankheiten, 117, 76-136.

Bacon, J., "Incel: What it is and why Alek Minassian praised Elliot Rodger," *USA Today*, April 25, 2018

BBC News, (2015) "Mother Tania Clarence who killed children 'overwhelmed'," BBC.com, 23, November 2015, https://www.bbc.com/news/uk-england-london-34898895

Bell, K. J. (2009). "A Feminist's Argument on How Sex Work Can Benefit Women." INQUIRIES JOURNAL/STUDENT PULSE, 1(11). Retrieved from http://www.inquiriesjournal.com/a?id=28

Bourget, D., Grace, J., & Whitehurst, L. (2007). A review of maternal and paternal filicide. *Journal-American Academy of Psychiatry and The Law*, *35*(1), 74.

Brodsky, C. M. (1976) The Harassed Worker, Lexington Books, DC Heath, Toronto.

Bruel N. & Luongo D. (2017) "Making It Safer: A Study of Law Enforcement
Fatalities Between 2010-2016" U.S. Department of Justice

California Digital Newspaper Collection. "One Teacher Killed, Two Wounded
When Youth Goes on Gun Rampage." Madera Tribune, Volume 64,
Number 302, 5 May 1956. Retrieved Feb 19, 2022 from
https://cdnc.ucr.edu/?a=d&d=MT19560505.2.18&e=-------en--20--1--txt-
txIN--------1

CDC FastStats: https://www.cdc.gov/nchs/fastats/homicide.htm

Chun S, Harris A, Carrion M, Rojas E, Stark S, Lejuez C, Lechner WV,
Bornovalova MA. A psychometric investigation of gender differences
and common processes across borderline and antisocial personality
disorders. J Abnorm Psychol. 2017 Jan;126(1):76-88. doi:
10.1037/abn0000220. Epub 2016 Nov 3. PMID: 27808543; PMCID:
PMC5217473.

Cleveland19.com, "TJ Lane Misbehaving Behind Bars" *Published: Feb. 2, 2016
at 12:55 PM PST* retrieved from
(https://www.cleveland19.com/story/31118545/chardon-school-shooter-
tj-lane-misbehaving-behind-bars-chillicothe/) on Feb 19, 2022

Davis, A. C., Vaillancourt, T., & Arnocky, S. (2020). The Dark Tetrad and Male
Clients of Female Sex Work. *Frontiers in psychology*, *11*, 577171.
https://doi.org/10.3389/fpsyg.2020.577171

DeMare, N. (2016). "Exaggerations and Stereotypes of Schizophrenia in
Contemporary Films." ELON JOURNAL OF UNDERGRADUATE
RESEARCH IN COMMUNICATIONS, 7(1). Retrieved
from http://www.inquiriesjournal.com/a?id=1474

Eisenberger, Naomi & Lieberman, Matthew & Williams, Kipling. (2003). Does Rejection Hurt? An fMRI Study of Social Exclusion. Science (New York, N.Y.). 302. 290-2. 10.1126/science.1089134.

Encyclopedia of Arkansas (https://encyclopediaofarkansas.net/entries/negro-boys-industrial-school-fire-of-1959-5500/)

Evans B. (2013). How autism became autism: The radical transformation of a central concept of child development in Britain. *History of the human sciences*, *26*(3), 3–31. https://doi.org/10.1177/0952695113484320

Farley, M., Golding, J. M., Matthews, E. S., Malamuth, N. M., & Jarrett, L. (2017). Comparing Sex Buyers with Men Who Do Not Buy Sex: New Data on Prostitution and Trafficking. Journal of Interpersonal Violence, 32(23), 3601–3625. https://doi.org/10.1177/0886260515600874

FBI: Uniform Crime Report, https://ucr.fbi.gov/crime-in-the-u.s/

FBI: "Serial Murder: Multidisciplinary Perspectives for Investigators" retrieved from https://www.fbi.gov/stats-services/publications/serial-murder#two on March 10, 2022

French Penal Code of 1810 (https://www.napoleon-series.org/research/government/france/penalcode/c_penalcode3b.html)

Gerbner, G., Gross, L., Morgan, M., & Signorielli, N. (1986). LIVING WITH TELEVISION: THE DYNAMICS OF THE CULTIVATION PROCESS. Perspectives on media effects, 1986, 17-40.

Gerbner, G., Gross, L., Morgan, M., & Signorielli, N. (1994). Growing up with television: The cultivation perspective.

Gershoff, E. T. (2002). Corporal punishment by parents and associated child behaviors and experiences: a meta-analytic and theoretical review. *Psychological bulletin, 128*(4), 539.

Goldner, L., Lev-Wiesel, R., & Simon, G. (2019). Revenge Fantasies After Experiencing Traumatic Events: Sex Differences. *Frontiers in psychology, 10*, 886. https://doi.org/10.3389/fpsyg.2019.00886

Harlow, H. F. (1958). The nature of love. AMERICAN PSYCHOLOGIST, 13(12), 673–685. https://doi.org/10.1037/h0047884

Hawes, D. J., & Dadds, M. R. (2005). The treatment of conduct problems in children with callous-unemotional traits. *Journal of consulting and clinical psychology, 73*(4), 737.

Heide, K.M. (2013). Understanding Parricide: When Sons and Daughters Kill Parents. Oxford: Oxford University Press.

Hermann, B.P., Seidenberg, M., Bell, B., Woodard, A., Rutecki, P., Sheth, R., "Comorbid psychiatric symptoms in temporal lobe epilepsy: association with chronicity of epilepsy and impact on quality of life." Epilepsy Behav, 1 (2000), pp. 184-190

Homeland Security, U.S. Fire Administration/Technical Report Series, "Special Report: Firefighter Arson "USFA-TR-141/January 2003

Howard, R. (2001). A Beautiful Mind. Universal Pictures.

Internet Movie Database (https://www.imdb.com/list/ls000092319/) retrieved March 4, 2022

Johnson, Alex (2018) "Parkland shooting suspect Nikolas Cruz spoke of 'voices,' says he attempted suicide" NBC News, retrieved May 2, 2022 from: https://www.nbcnews.com/news/us-news/parkland-shooting-suspect-nikolas-cruz-spoke-voices-says-he-attempted-n898151

Kanner, L. (1943). Autistic disturbances of affective contact. *Nervous Child* 2, 217-250.

Kappel, A., Lasola, W. (Producers) "Ted Bundy: The Survivors" (TV Miniseries), October 2020.

Kendall, Elizabeth (1981). *The Phantom Prince: My Life with Ted Bundy.* Abrams &Chronicle Books. ISBN 978-1419744853

Kumari, A. "Psychoanalysis of postpartum in the yellow wallpaper and breaking point." Sparkling International Journal of Multidisciplinary Research Studies Vol.2, Issue.3, July – September 2019

LeRoy, M. (Director). (1956). *The Bad Seed* [Film]. Warner Brothers.

Masters, Brian (1993). *The Shrine of Jeffrey Dahmer.* London, England: Hodder & Stoughton. ISBN 978-0-340-59194-9(https://books.google.com/books?id=g3 1XGwAACAAJ)

Meerwijk EL, Ford JM, Weiss SJ. Brain regions associated with psychological pain: implications for a neural network and its relationship to physical pain. Brain Imaging Behav. 2013 Mar;7(1):1-14. doi: 10.1007/s11682-012-9179-y. PMID: 22660945.

Michaud, Stephen G., and Hugh Aynesworth (2000). *Ted Bundy: Conversations with a Killer.* Authorlink Press. ISBN 978-1928704-17-1

Milgram, S. (1974). Obedience to authority: An experimental view. New York: Harper & Row.

Myers, Wade C.; Gooch, Erik; Meloy, J. Reid (2005). "The Role of Psychopathy and Sexuality in a Female Serial Killer". *Journal of Forensic Sciences*. **50** (3): 652–7.

Najib A, Lorberbaum JP, Kose S, Bohning DE, George MS. Regional brain activity in women grieving a romantic relationship breakup. Am J Psychiatry. 2004 Dec;161(12):2245-56. doi: 10.1176/appi.ajp.161.12.2245. PMID: 15569896.

Nasar, S. (2002). *A Beautiful Mind*. Faber & Faber.

National Center on Shaken Baby Syndrome, "Shaken Baby Syndrome?" (https://www.dontshake.org/)

News Corps. "Woman most intimate with theater shooter before massacre testifies" College of Media, Communication, and Information, University of Colorado Boulder, posted June 10, 2015. Retrieved April 2, 2022 from https://www.colorado.edu/initiative/newscorps/2015/06/10/woman-most-intimate-theater-shooter-massacre-testifies

Newton, M. (2006). *The encyclopedia of serial killers*. Infobase Publishing.

Nisbett, R. E., & Ross, L. D. Human inference: Strategies and shortcomings of social judgment. Englewood Cliffs, N.J.: Prentice-Hall, 1980.

Norris, Joel (1992). *Jeffrey Dahmer*. London, England: Constable & Robinson. ISBN 978-0-09-472060-2.(https://www.google.co.uk/books/edition/Jeffrey_Dahme r/mDekPAAACAAJ)

O'Hern D. (2017). "An Analysis of Bipolar Disorder Stereotypes in 21st Century Television Programming." *Elon Journal of Undergraduate Research in Communications,* 8(2), 67-76

Owens D, Horrocks J, and House A. Fatal and non-fatal repetition of self-harm: systematic review. British Journal of Psychiatry. 2002; 181:193-199.

Palermo MT, Bogaerts S. The Dangers of Posthumous Diagnoses and the Unintended Consequences of Facile Associations: Jeffrey Dahmer and Autism Spectrum Disorders. Int J Offender Ther Comp Criminol. 2015 Dec;59(14):1564-79. doi: 10.1177/0306624X14550642. Epub 2014 Sep 10. PMID: 25209624.

Peterson J, Densley J, Erickson G. Presence of Armed School Officials and Fatal and Nonfatal Gunshot Injuries During Mass School Shootings, United States, 1980-2019. JAMA NETW OPEN. 2021;4(2): e2037394. doi:10.1001/jamanetworkopen.2020.37394

Resnick PJ. Child murder by parents: A psychiatric review of filicide. *Am J Psychiatry.* 1969; 126:325-34. [PubMed: 5801251]

Resnick PJ. Filicide in the United States. *Indian J Psychiatry.* 2016 Dec; (Suppl2): S203-S209

Spencer, Suzy "Breaking Point" Diversion Books (October 20, 2015)

Rieber, R. W. (2006). THE BIFURCATION OF THE SELF: THE HISTORY AND THEORY OF DISSOCIATION AND ITS DISORDERS. Springer Science + Business Media. https://doi.org/10.1007/0-387-27414-6

Richard-Devantoy S, Olie JP, Gourevitch R. [Risk of homicide and major mental disorders: a critical review]. L'encephale. 2009 Dec;35(6):521-530. DOI: 10.1016/j.encep.2008.10.009. PMID: 20004282.

Rule, Ann (1980). *The Stranger Beside Me.* W.W. Norton and Company Inc. ISBN 978-1-938402-78-4

Sajous-Turner, A., Anderson, N.E., Widdows, M. *et al.* Aberrant brain gray matter in murderers. *Brain Imaging and Behavior* **14,** 2050–2061 (2020). https://doi.org/10.1007/s11682-019-00155-y

Santiago, Ellyn, "Eric Harris' Parents & Brother, Wayne, Kathy & Kevin Harris: 5 Fast Facts You Need to Know" Heavy.com, published April 16, 2019, retrieved May 02, 2022 from: https://heavy.com/news/2019/04/eric-harris-parents-brother-wayne-kathy-kevin-harris/

Schneiderman I, Zagoory-Sharon O, Leckman JF, Feldman R. Oxytocin during the initial stages of romantic attachment: relations to couples' interactive reciprocity. Psychoneuroendocrinology. (2012) 37:1277–85. doi: 10.1016/j.psyneuen.2011.12.021

Schreiber, F. R. (1974). *Sybil.* New York, N.Y: Warner Books.

Silva JA, Ferrari MM, Leong GB. The case of Jeffrey Dahmer: sexual serial homicide from a neuropsychiatric developmental perspective. J Forensic Sci. 2002 Nov;47(6):1347-59. PMID: 12455663.

Skakoon-Sparling S, Cramer KM, Shuper PA. The Impact of Sexual Arousal on Sexual Risk-Taking and Decision-Making in Men and Women. Arch Sex Behav. 2016 Jan;45(1):33-42. doi: 10.1007/s10508-015-0589-y. Epub 2015 Aug 27. PMID: 26310879.

Spelman, W. How Cohorts Changed Crime Rates, 1980–2016. *J Quant Criminol* (2021). https://doi.org/10.1007/s10940-021-09508-7

"Spiegelgrund Survivors Speak Out". *War Against the Inferior*. Steinhof Memorial. Retrieved 2 March 2022. (http://gedenkstaettesteinhof.at/en/interview)

State of Washington vs. Gary Leon Ridgway; King County Prosecutor's Office. November 2003. Archived from the original (PDF) on January 5, 2015. Retrieved March 11, 2022 – via The Seattle Times.

Stopbullying.gov (https://www.stopbullying.gov/resources/facts) retrieved Feb 13, 2022

Taylor, Steve "The Jumpers: What happens when a person survives jumping off the Golden Gate Bridge?" Psychology Today (Sept 29, 2011) Retrieved from https://www.psychologytoday.com/us/blog/out-the-darkness/201109/the-jumpers

Texas Public Radio (2017) "Evidence Destroyed In Hospital Cover-Up Needed In Genene Jones Prosecution" Author David Martin Davies, published July 12, 2017, retrieved from https://www.tpr.org/news/2017-07-12/evidence-destroyed-in-hospital-cover-up-needed-in-genene-jones-prosecution

The Iceman - Confessions of a Mafia Hitman (DVD). HBO. June 1, 2004. (https://www.hbo.com/documentaries/catalog.th e-iceman-confesses-secrets-of-a-mafia-hitman)

Ulibarri MD, Hiller SP, Lozada R, Rangel MG, Stockman JK, Silverman JG, Ojeda VD. "Prevalence and characteristics of abuse experiences and depression symptoms among injection drug-using female sex workers in Mexico." J Environ Public Health. 2013;2013:631479. doi: 10.1155/2013/631479. Epub 2013 May 12. PMID: 23737808; PMCID: PMC3666207.

United States Department of Justice: Office of Justice Programs
(https://www.ojp.gov/ncjrs/virtual-library/abstracts/serial-
murder#:~:text=Four%20types%20of%20serial%20murderers,'power%2
Fcontrol%2Doriented.)

Valeria Abreu Minero, Edward Barker, Rachael Bedford, Method of homicide and
severe mental illness: A systematic review, Aggression and Violent
Behavior, Volume 37, 2017, Pages 52-62, ISSN 1359-1789.

Vicary AM, Fraley RC. Captured by True Crime: Why Are Women Drawn to
Tales of Rape, Murder, and Serial Killers? Social Psychological and
Personality Science. 2010;1(1):81-86. doi:10.1177/1948550609355486

Viner, R. M., Booy, R., Johnson, H., Edmunds, W. J., Hudson, L., Bedford, H., ...
& Christie, D. (2012). Outcomes of invasive meningococcal serogroup B
disease in children and adolescents (MOSAIC): a case-control study. *The
Lancet Neurology*, *11*(9), 774-783.

Violence Policy Center, 2020. "AMERICAN ROULETTE: MURDER-SUICIDE
IN THE UNITED STATES" retrieved from
https://vpc.org/studies/amroul2020.pdf on 02/25/2022.

Wallace, Maeve PhD; Gillispie-Bell, Veronica MD; Cruz, Kiara MPH; Davis,
Kelly MPA; Vilda, Dovile PhD Homicide During Pregnancy and the
Postpartum Period in the United States, 2018–2019, Obstetrics &
Gynecology: November 2021 - Volume 138 - Issue 5 - p 762-769 doi:
10.1097/AOG.0000000000004567

Wallman, B., McMahon, P., O'Matz, M., & Bryan, S., (2018), "A Lost and Lonely Killer" South Florida Sun-Sentinel -- Feb 24, 2018, retrieved May 2, 2022 from https://www.sun-sentinel.com/local/broward/parkland/florida-school-shooting/fl-florida-school-shooting-nikolas-cruz-life-20180220-story.html

Watson, J. B. (1930). Behaviorism (Revised Edition). Chicago, IL: University of Chicago Press.

Waxman SG, Geschwind N. The Interictal Behavior Syndrome of Temporal Lobe Epilepsy. ARCH GEN PSYCHIATRY. 1975;32(12):1580–1586. doi:10.1001/archpsyc.1975.01760300118011

Zhang, X., Ge, T. T., Yin, G., Cui, R., Zhao, G., & Yang, W. (2018). Stress-Induced Functional Alterations in Amygdala: Implications for Neuropsychiatric Diseases. *Frontiers in neuroscience*, *12*, 367. https://doi.org/10.3389/fnins.2018.00367

About the author

Casey Lytle teaches psychology and sociology with specialties in deception, murder, and conspiracy theories. While at Eastern Washington University he taught special-topic classes in Psychology of Deception and Psychology of Murder. While teaching deception he introduced the "project management" approach to placing conspiracy theories on a spectrum from rational to irrational, and while teaching Psychology of Murder began emphasizing the ways murderers are similar to us and how "every day" people are responsible for the majority of murders each year.

Casey lives in a haunted house in the Pacific Northwest with his son and a collection of creepy dolls who only sometimes move around in the night.

Bibliography

Lytle, C. (September 27, 2022) *Debunked: Separate the rational from the irrational in influential conspiracy theories*. Penguin Random House.